ALBERTA'S
Weekly
NEWSPAPERS

Writing the First Draft of History

Wayne Arthurson

Alberta
Weekly Newspapers
Association

The Publisher: Folklore Publishing in cooperation with the Alberta Weekly Newspapers Association
Website: www.folklorepublishing.com

Library and Archives Canada Cataloguing in Publication

Arthurson, Wayne, 1962–
Alberta's weekly newspapers: writing the first draft of history / Wayne Arthurson. —1st ed.

ISBN 978-1-926677-80-4

1. Alberta—History. 2. Canadian newspapers (English)—
Alberta—History. I. Title.

FC3661.A77 2012   971.23   C2012-900563-0

Project Director: Faye Boer
Project Editor: Kathy van Denderen
Cover Images: Courtesy of several of the Alberta Weekly Newspapers featured in this volume: The Capital—Three Hills, Claresholm Local Press, The Community Press—Flagstaff County, The High River Times, The Hub—Hay River, The Lamont Leader, Mayerthorpe Freelancer, The Nanton News, Spruce Grove Examiner, St. Albert Gazette, The Stony Plain Reporter, The Tofield Mercury, Vermillion Standard, The Weekly Review—Viking.

Photo Credits: Every effort has been made to accurately credit the sources of photographs. Any errors or omissions should be reported directly to the publisher for correction in future editions. Photographs courtesy of Athabasca Archives (p. 95, 1246c); Glenbow Museum (p. 11, ND-3-7137; p. 13, NA-433-5; p. 20, NA-659-73; p. 25, NA-937-12; p. 30, PA-3520-826, PA-3520-823; p. 34, NA-67-28; p. 35, PA-3520-242; p. 36, NA-460-33; p. 41, NA-476-1; p. 42, NA-3685-11; p. 69, NA-2127-4; p. 81, NA-1912-2; p. 87, NA-2127-5; p. 108, ND-2-122; p. 122, NA-1170-4; p. 132, NC-54-1972; p. 161, IP-6f-18; p. 178, NC-29-56; p. 180, NA-489-4; p. 211, PA-2025-11); Library and Archives Canada (p. 77, PA-025025); Library of Congress (p. 45, LC-USF34-060410D); Provincial Archives of Alberta (pp. 84, 115, 170); Saskatoon Public Library–Local History Room (p. 46, PH-87-103; p. 50, PH-87-100). All other photographs courtesy of the Alberta Weekly Newspapers Association and its members.

Produced with the assistance of the Government of Alberta, **Government** Alberta Multimedia Development Fund **of Alberta** ■

This project was funded in part by the Alberta Historical Resources Foundation.

We acknowledge the financial support of the Government of Canada through the Canada Book Fund (CBF) for our publishing activities.

 Canadian   Patrimoine
Heritage   canadien

PC: 1

Contents

Acknowledgements

First, I must thank the Board of Directors, staff and member newspapers of the Alberta Weekly Newspapers Association, especially Executive Director Dennis Merrell and publishers George Brown, Richard Holmes and Frank McTighe.

Also thanks to Faye Boer and Folklore Publishing for making the publication of this book possible, and to my editor Kathy van Denderen.

Further thanks must go to the staff at the Edmonton Public Library, the Alberta Legislative Library, the City of Edmonton Archive, the Provincial Archives of Alberta and the Glenbow Museum Archives. Their assistance was invaluable in the research for this book.

And finally, thanks to all the Alberta newspaper publishers, editors, reporters and other staff, past and present, for their role in the life and history of Alberta.

Other Contributors

The following people contributed the individual newspaper histories that appear in the sidebars throughout this book.

Kerry Anderson	R.C.R. Munro
Brian Bachynski	Jamie Nesbitt
Chris Brodeur	Lorraine Poulsen
Amber Cowie	Bev Rudolfsen
Bill Holmes	Mike Scott
Duff Jamison	Jay Shearlaw
Shaun Jessome	Tim Shearlaw
Dennis Merrell	Rob Vogt
Nancy Middleton	

Introduction

In May 1987, I began my professional writing career. I was hired as the reporter/photographer for the *Olds Gazette*. The paper was published by Neil Leatherdale, who had been running it since the end of World War II, taking it over from his father-in-law William Miller. By the time I had arrived, the *Gazette* had been in operation for 83 years.

At first, Leatherdale seemed like a tough old publisher, and in many ways he was. He was a veteran of World War II; I don't know if he ever saw action in the early part of the war, but I do know that he trained pilots in southern Alberta. Neil was also one of the few members of the Liberal Party in a Conservative town. He was a hard-nosed businessman who ran a tight newspaper and printing business, and he didn't suffer fools lightly.

For the most part, I wasn't one of those fools. Even from my first day, he pretty much gave me free rein in what I would write about. He would nudge me in certain directions, but by giving me the freedom to discover what was important to the town and its residents, he allowed me to become a member of that community on my own.

The paper itself harkened back to an older time. By the late 1980s, many community newspapers had made the transition to computers and desktop publishing. Most didn't even print their own papers, relying on centralized shops that contracted out those services. A lot of them were also tabloids, which were cheaper to print and mail out to subscribers.

The *Olds Gazette* was an old broadsheet, several inches wider than the daily broadsheets in Calgary and Edmonton. It printed the paper in a three-unit web press that usually ran on Mondays and Tuesdays, and sometimes on Fridays if there was a larger issue that week. My desk was less than 10 feet from that noisy machine, and I had to conduct phone interviews and write stories while it ran. Because of that experience, I now have the ability to write anywhere, regardless of noise.

I spent two years at the *Olds Gazette*, and two more down the street at the *Didsbury Review*. What I learned about writing, journalism and community in that time has never left me. I discovered that a community newspaper isn't just a font of information or a chronicle of events such as town council decisions, car accidents or sports results. Unlike the average daily newspaper or other big city media, the local weekly newspaper is an actual member of the community it serves. It not only supports the community by being the only supplier of local news, but it can also influence public opinion, galvanize a community about specific issues and figure in the history of the area, be it local or otherwise.

This book shows how weekly newspapers in Alberta responded to major and minor historical events since the first issue of the *Edmonton Bulletin* was published even before Alberta became a province. And through their words and actions, the papers became part of that history and helped shape the future of the province.

Author's Note

Throughout this book, I have taken text from various Alberta newspapers to reflect their response, opinion and attitude toward certain historical events. Many times, these pieces did not have bylines so there was no way to confirm the author. However, I did note the dates and the name of the newspaper in which they appeared.

You may also notice the typos, spelling mistakes, grammatical errors and the arcane and unusual use of language in many of the pieces. This is by design. Every piece of text from a newspaper in this book is reprinted the way it was the first time it appeared in the local newspaper. This was done not to highlight the fact that sometimes newspapers make mistakes or that journalists and publishers had a quaint way of writing in the past but to keep the purity of the voice of the original writer, so that you, as the reader, will read exactly what the members of the community read in their newspaper at the time it was printed.

CHAPTER ONE

The Arrival of the Weekly

THE ALBERTA NEWSPAPER INDUSTRY was born on December 6, 1880. The *Edmonton Bulletin* may not have been the first newspaper to appear in Alberta—no doubt many residents had subscriptions for papers from the eastern provinces—but the *Bulletin* was the first newspaper of any kind to be solely written, edited and printed in the western Canadian territory.

At the time of the paper's first edition, Alberta was two decades from becoming a province and was still only a part of the larger North-West Territories. Edmonton was just a hamlet of settlements gathered around the Hudson's Bay Company's Fort with a population of approximately 300. All along the banks of the North Saskatchewan River, homesteaders farmed strips of land.

The editor of the *Edmonton Bulletin* was Frank Oliver, a 27-year-old former apprentice printer, also known as a "printer's devil." Originally from Peel County, Ontario, he was born Frank Bowsfield in 1853, the son of a farmer, but during his teenaged years, he had a disagreement with his father and by the time he graduated high school, he assumed his mother's maiden name as his own. After high school, he moved to Toronto to set type for the *Toronto Globe*. While at the *Globe*, Oliver read stories about the growth of Western Canada and the potential there for young men with ambition and a strong work ethic.

Enthused with the possibilities, he left the *Globe* and headed west, settling in Winnipeg. After three years of working for the *Winnipeg Free Press*, Oliver began hearing rumours about the construction of a trans-Canada railway. The rumours, which turned out to be incorrect, stated that the new railway would stop within a few miles of Fort Edmonton. Young Frank Oliver decided that Edmonton was the place to be. So in 1876, he loaded up a Red River cart with goods, mostly bacon and flour, and joined an ox train whose ultimate destination was a sawmill 80 kilometres upriver of the fort.

At a spot where the University of Alberta now stands, Oliver departed the train, set up his tent and worked on a plan to get his goods across the river where most of the population resided. In a short time, he built a raft and pushed off the south bank of the river, bound for the north. Unfortunately, Oliver's raft capsized, and he lost much of his cargo. Even so, he managed to survive the crossing and, with the leftovers, set up Oliver Cartage and Dry Goods Shop, the first privately owned retail store in Edmonton outside of the Hudson's Bay trading post. Over the next few years, Oliver made several trips between Fort Edmonton and Winnipeg, transporting and shipping goods that people needed or had ordered.

One of the ways Oliver attracted people to his store was to post telegraphed news items on the walls. He got the information from Alex Taylor, the local telegraph operator.

Like Oliver, Taylor was a former Ontario native transplanted west. Born in Ottawa in 1854, Taylor was the son of a railway engineer and sometimes accompanied his father on his regular Ottawa to Prescott run. In 1879, at the age of 25, Taylor was hired by a government telegraph contractor to relieve the local operator in Hay River. Not long after he arrived in the town, members of the fledging community of Edmonton lobbied the federal government to relocate the telegraph office to their

Edmonton Bulletin newsboys' bus, 1935

∽

village. By January 1880, Taylor was a resident of Edmonton, first living in temporary quarters on John Walter's land on the south side of the river, and then later to a permanent office on the north side of the river.

When Oliver and Taylor realized that many of the residents of the area came into the store just to read the news items posted on the wall, they hatched an idea.

Taylor used his telegraph connections to find a small printing press in Minneapolis or Philadelphia (the exact location is not known) and arranged to have it shipped to Winnipeg. Frank Oliver picked up the printing press during one his trips for goods in late 1880 and brought it to Edmonton. The press weighed 90 kilograms and cost $20.

On December 6, 1880, the first edition of the *Edmonton Bulletin* was printed and distributed. It was small, five by seven inches, and only four pages. The first and subsequent issues in the paper's early years featured the same type of telegraphic news that Oliver had pasted on the walls of his store, plus a variety of local announcements and notices that would become a staple of the Alberta weekly for decades.

The river is still open in places.

Capt. Herchmer is expected at Fort Saskatchewan shortly.

James Yorker of Fort Saskatchewan killed a black bear lately.

Mr. Wm Rowland, who was very sick last week, is recovering.

Telegraph Line commenced working again on Wed.

Mr. J Favel, pilot, Str; lily, arrived from Victoria Wednesday.

The case Annand vs McLeod was adjourned indefinitely on Thursday.

H. Allison, of Fort Saskatchewan shot 100 prairie chickens in one day last week.

Dr. Verey has bought Ed MacPherson's claim near Edmonton for one hundred dollars.

The Indian Department will ship to Victoria 6000 lbs of beef for the Indians.

The police at Fort Saskatchewan complain that they have not been paid for three months.

–*Edmonton Bulletin*, December 13, 1880

There is an unconfirmed story that before the release of the first edition of the *Edmonton Bulletin*, the large pieces of type Oliver and Taylor had purchased for the masthead were damaged in some way. So Alex Taylor carved the *Edmonton Bulletin* masthead out of a piece of wood, and they used that for several months until Patrick Gammie Laurie, the publisher and founder of the *Saskatchewan Herald* (the first newspaper

Frank Oliver, founder of the *Edmonton Bulletin*

in the North-West Territories located in Battleford) offered them some extra pieces of type.

Less than a year after the first edition, Alex Taylor lost interest in the paper and focused more on his homestead. Still, he played a key role in the continued development of Edmonton. Taylor not only became one of the most important and knowledgeable farmers in the area, but he also founded the first telephone exchange, the first local Presbyterian Church, the first electric company and the local Masonic lodge.

As for Frank Oliver, he found his calling in the *Bulletin*. He saw the paper's articles and advertising as not only a way to provide information to the community and promote local projects and businesses but also a means to champion Alberta's second largest municipality.

Partly because of the *Bulletin*, Frank Oliver became one of the most important and influential citizens in Edmonton and in Alberta. Edmonton had been dealt a tough blow when it was bypassed in favour of Calgary for the first trans-Canada railway, the Canadian Pacific Railway. But Oliver vowed never to let Edmonton be second best again. He was a strong opponent of taxation without representation, and his editorials consistently lashed out at the federal government in Ottawa.

> *The royalty rate of one dollar per ton on coal mined in the North West is another case of simple robbery. The future settlers of the North West will have to use coal almost entirely and why should they have to pay towards the revenue this tax over and above what the residents of other provinces pay? It is not to prevent waste, for the supply can never become exhausted. It is simply a fine that a man has to pay for coming into the North West. Let it be remembered that while the coal here pays a royalty of $1 a ton, that of Nova Scotia is protected to the extent of 50 cents a ton.*
>
> *Why is it that the members of the Government have racked their brains to find new things to tax in the North West. It is to curry favour with those narrow-minded ones in the Eastern Provinces who consider the North West a bill of expense, and to prove to them that they know how to make it pay.*
>
> *–Edmonton Bulletin*, date unknown, 1881

Because of his strong feelings about the West and who should represent it, Oliver ran as an independent Liberal in 1896 and was elected to office. He was an MP until 1921, serving as Minster of the Interior and Superintendent of Indians. When Alberta became a province in 1905, Prime Minister Wilfrid Laurier's confidence in Oliver was credited, rightly or wrongly, with Edmonton being chosen as the province's capital. Edmontonians loved Oliver for it; Calgarians hated him.

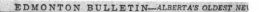

A photograph from the *Edmonton Bulletin*, January 18, 1936. Top row (left to right): C.L. Dunford (*Sylvan Lake News*), F.P. Galbraith (*Red Deer Advocate*), R.C. Jessup (*MacLeod Gazette*), W. Conquest (*Athabasca Echo*), W.H. Betts (*Hughenden Record*). Bottom row: G.C. Duncan (*Drumheller Mail*), H.G. Thunell (*Viking News*), Herb McCrea (*Hanna Herald*), H.T. Halliwell (*Coleman Journal*)

The *Calgary Herald* called the *Bulletin* "the meanest paper published by the meanest man in Canada." Although that reaction was because of Oliver's role in getting Edmonton named as Alberta's capital city, some of it was partly true. As the Minister of the Interior, Oliver was responsible for immigration, and he made no bones about what nationality of immigrants he preferred: English or Scottish. Even at a time when public sentiment toward Natives and Eastern European immigrants was quite negative, Oliver's comments about these groups were considered racist.

While he served in Ottawa, Oliver still kept the *Bulletin* going. In time, it became a daily, and along with the *Edmonton Journal,* was one of two to serve Edmonton in the first half of the 20th century. In 1951, the *Edmonton Bulletin* ceased publication.

~

CHAPTER TWO

Southern Reply

FOR TWO YEARS AFTER ITS FIRST EDITION was released, the *Edmonton Bulletin* was Alberta's only locally produced newspaper. In 1882, a new player arrived on the scene in the southern region of the province at Fort Macleod, a location that many looking back on Alberta's history would not expect.

Fort Macleod is named after Colonel James F. Macleod, the second commissioner of the North-West Mounted Police (NWMP) and a key figure in the European settlement of Canada's west. In 1874, Macleod led a procession of 150 members of the NWMP west to put an end to the illegal whisky trade into the North-West Territory from the United States. On the banks of the Oldman River, not far from Fort Whoop-Up, the notorious whisky trading post, Macleod and his men set up camp. Later, they established Fort Macleod and dismantled Fort Whoop-Up and the whisky trade.

Charles E.D. Wood and E.T. "Si" Saunders were two of Fort Macleod's original battalion of mounted police. On July 1, 1882, after mustering out of the NWMP, the two men set up an office in a 10-by-12-foot tent with a dirt floor and a mud roof, which when it rained outside, water dripped from the roof for days afterward. The pair founded the *Macleod Gazette*, now the longest-running newspaper in Alberta history.

The *Macleod Gazette* building in the 1890s. Editor Charles E.D. Wood is on the left. The man on the right is unknown.

"It is perhaps needless to say that the birth of the *Gazette* was celebrated. We needed mighty little encouragement in those days. Celebrations all looked alike to us. Old Kamoose kept open house and D.W. Davis dispensed liquid refreshments," Wood wrote later. "Tony Lachapelle got one of the first copies of the *Gazette* printed, and went to bed early that night, so that he would be sure to get everything there was in the paper before morning. Joe Carr bought ten copies, and retired to the privacy of the Bulls Head Market, where he read each one of them four times, and was not seen for three or four days. Dick Kennefick led the artillery brigade and fired off the anvils, only four of his helpers being seriously maimed, while the rest lost parts of their hair and whiskers.

"And so the *Gazette* was launched on the troubled sea of journalism, and there has been more or less trouble ever since."

The front page of the first edition was mostly boilerplate (reprinted material), featuring the poem "A Valentine" by R.O.F. and a story about a parrot. The edition also featured a "Salutation" by the new publishers.

> *Owing to the rapid increase of settlers and large stock owners in the Bow River district, it became evident that a newspaper was not only much needed, but an absolute necessity, as a means of conveying accurate and minute information to intending immigrants, and of advancing the interests and giving a voice to those already settled here—to those who have broken the ice and opened up the many resources of the country to the world. This idea became gradually infused throughout the district, resulting in the establishment of the GAZETTE, the first issue of which we now launch upon the sea of public opinion, trusting that its fate may not be to founder among the rocks and shoals which it is sure to pass, but that it may steer its course safely through those bugbears of navigation, landing, what we shall always endeavor to have, its cargo of good, reliable and instructing lore in the harbour of its destination, success, the advancement of our country and the happiness and prosperity of its people.*

–*Macleod Gazette,* July 1, 1882

The two ex-Mounties ran the *Gazette* as a team, with Wood handling the editorial and Saunders dealing with the typesetting and printing. It became so successful that three years later, in 1885, they branched out. Saunders moved to Lethbridge and under the same partnership, launched the *Lethbridge News*, which was printed at the office in Fort Macleod. A year later, however, the two partners swapped shares in their respective newspapers and the *Macleod Gazette* and *Lethbridge News* operated as separate entities.

Saunders was with the *Lethbridge News* until 1900, at which time he moved to Pincher Creek to found the *Rocky Mountain Echo*. In 1906,

Charles E.D. Wood, publisher of the *Macleod Gazette*, 1888

he changed the name to the *Pincher Creek Echo*—the paper and the name still exist today—and operated the paper until his death on January 9, 1920.

As a note of interest, a local lawyer named Fred Haultain wrote editorials that appeared in the *Lethbridge News*. Haultain became historically known as the Honourable Sir Frederick W.A.G. Haultain, the first and only premier of the North-West Territories, from 1897 to 1905.

Following the break-up of the original Saunders-Wood partnership, the *Macleod Gazette* changed hands several times. Wood left the paper to study law, leaving the publication in the capable hands of Thomas and F. Clarke, two brothers who ran the short-lived *Macleod Advertiser* in 1907. Wood returned to the *Gazette* in 1894, but left again because of his election to the North-West Territories Assembly, leasing the paper to Zachary Hamilton. Hamilton would later work as a journalist for the *Regina Leader-Post*.

Following his term in the assembly, Wood returned to the *Gazette*, but in 1903 he left the paper for good, moving to Regina to become a partner in a law firm. Following his departure, the *Gazette* went through a series of owners and even disappeared for almost 25 years in 1907. In 1931, Ralph C. Jessup took over the operation of the *Macleod Times* and changed its name to the *Fort Macleod Gazette*. The Jessup family owned the paper until 1975. The paper went through several changes in ownership and is currently owned by Frank and Emily McTighe.

> *The history of the* Gazette *is practically the history of southern Alberta, and to a very great extent the whole of the North West Territories. The* Gazette *saw the foundation of the great range cattle and horse business, and has lived to see it develop into one of the most important industries in the Dominion, until now when it is fast being crowded back by the rapidly advancing tide of settlement. From a little hamlet of log huts with mud floors and the grass growing out of the earth which covered the roofs, the* Gazette *has witnessed the steady growth of Macleod, until is has become a large and thriving town with substantial business blocks and handsome residences. In those days there were no railways, no schools, no post offices and practically no representative government. Now railways traverse the country in all directions, there are hundreds of schools, and every settlement has its post office and mail service. The changes in all those twenty-one years has indeed been marvelous and bit by bit it has been recorded in the* Gazette.
>
> –Charles Wood's final editorial,
> *Macleod Gazette*, July 3, 1903

THE HUB

On February 15, 1973, the first issue of *The Hub* hit Hay River's streets.

With hand-drawn ads and the only colour a splotch of yellow on the front page, the newspaper wasn't much to look at by today's standards, but it was history in the making.

That first issue covered topics ranging from a proposed high rise for the community (it's now the town's landmark) to a student sit-in at Diamond Jenness on the school's opening day—they were upset because there was no smoking area (some issues never go away).

The issue also contained a welcome to the new paper, in which the publishers wrote: "We won't pull any punches in reporting accurately the workings of Town Council, but neither will we conduct private feuds with any level of government. We'll give you the facts, you figure out the rest.

"This is a COMMUNITY newspaper, it is about you and for you; we want and need to know your opinion on anything that affects your life."

The newspaper has been owned by publisher Chris Brodeur for most of its existence. However, *The Hub* was not Hay River's first newspaper.

In the early days of Hay River, a number of small gazette-type flyers were distributed in the community, and the *Mackenzie Press* and *Hay River Optimist* were published here.

But the first step to a truly Hay River newspaper was actually made in, of all places, Fort Smith. That's where Boreal Press, headed by Don Taylor and Jim Whelly, started *Tapwe*, which covered the news in the Mackenzie District, in northern Alberta and Saskatchewan. It included stories from the CP wire, including, in the first edition, April 9, 1963, the election of Lester B. Pearson as prime minister.

It was a rough year for newspapers. Both the *Mackenzie Press* and the *Hay River Optimist* ceased operations that year, the latter because of the death of its publisher Jock McMeekan. *Tapwe* closed in Fort Smith in September of that same year, but then, on January 23, 1964, it reopened in Hay River, with Don Taylor as the sole owner.

"Hay River appears to offer a firmer footing for our type of operation," Taylor wrote. "It seems to have a good printing and advertising potential and has every appearance of being the boom town of the North."

After almost 18 years and 900 issues, the final edition of *Tapwe* under Taylor and Boreal Press was published on February 25, 1981.

MacWeston Press, under Vicky Latour and Heidi MacLeod, took over the operation. A few months later, on May 6, *Tapwe* switched from the 8.25" × 10.75" pony tab to an 11" × 17" tabloid. Latour soon become the sole owner of *Tapwe*.

In the meantime, on February 15, 1973, the first issue of *The Hub* rolled off the presses.

Published and edited by Harry and Pat Engbers of North of 60 Publications, *The Hub* was a 28-page pony tab but on August 15, 1973, switched to the tab format.

In 1972, Chris Brodeur joined *Tapwe* as assistant editor. In September 1974, he was lured over to *The Hub* from *Tapwe*. In May 1975, under the name Hub Publications Ltd., Brodeur purchased *The Hub* from the Engbers, who moved to BC.

The final edition of *Tapwe* under Latour was published in 1982, with Brodeur's Hub Publications Ltd. purchasing *Tapwe* on July 31, 1982. Latour later accepted Brodeur's offer to work as editor for *The Hub*.

Latour continued to work with *The Hub* for a number of years. Brodeur eventually began to spend more time in Alberta, and Sean Percy took the lead as managing editor. Percy guided the transition to publishing in full colour in 2000. In October 2011, Northern News Services purchased *The Hub* from Brodeur and continues to publish the paper every Wednesday. Northern News Services is owned by longtime northerners Jack Sigvaldason and Michael Scott. They publish *NWT News North, Yellowknifer, Deh Cho Drum* and *Inuvik Drum* in the Northwest Territories and *Nunavut News North* and *Kivalliq News* in Nunavut.

CHAPTER THREE

Eye-opening Times

WHEN THE *WETASKIWIN FREE LANCE* printed its first issue on March 26, 1897, it marked the first newspaper located between Calgary and Edmonton. By then, other newspapers had begun to grow in the province. Some of them were successful, such as the *Weekly Herald* in Calgary and the *Lethbridge News*, while others such as the *National Park Life* (Banff) and the *Nor'Wester* (Calgary) barely lasted a year.

The *Wetaskiwin Free Lance* soon joined the ranks of the short-lived. But the paper marked the arrival of one of the most unique newspaper publishers and editors in Alberta and one of the most colourful characters in Canadian history.

Bob Edwards was born in Glasgow, Scotland, on September 12, 1864. His maternal grandfather had founded a publishing company, and Edwards later said that if his mother had been a man, she too would have been in the publishing business. Unfortunately, Edwards' mother died a few weeks after his birth. His father passed on before Bob's fourth birthday.

Despite being orphaned at such a young age, Edwards received a solid education and wound up at Glasgow University. He did not care for the educational establishment and preferred playing pranks and socializing over classes. Upon graduation, one professor called him "a rebel with traits

Robert "Bob" C. Edwards, editor of the *Eye Opener*, Calgary, 1915

of literary genius." After university, he, like many other young gentlemen of the age, toured the continent, ending up in the south of France. There he took his first steps in the world of journalism, publishing the *Travel-ler*, an English-language newspaper catering to British gentry travelling abroad.

The paper was modestly successful, but Edwards soon tired of the society set and was looking for more adventure in his life. Along with his brother James, he moved to the American West and, despite their lack of experience, they found work on a cattle ranch in Wyoming. They spent 10 years in Wyoming, and after a barnyard mishap, in which Bob mistakenly attempted to milk a mule instead of a cow and ended up unconscious on the floor for three hours, he decided it was time to move on. North was the suggested way to go, and after a few months, Edwards arrived in Wetaskiwin with no money and no prospects.

After experiencing a few more bumps along the way, Edwards came up with the idea of a weekly newspaper, at first suggesting it be named Wetaskiwin Bottling Works. After negotiating a deal with the *Strathcona Plaindealer* to handle the printing, the more respectably named *Wetaskiwin Free Lance* was launched on March 26, 1897.

The paper's first office was a desk and a chair in the waiting room of the local livery stable. Compared to other newspapers of the day—the *Bulletin* in Edmonton and the *Weekly Herald* in Calgary—the *Free Lance* was shocking. Edwards was not interested in producing the same type of news that other papers were offering: boilerplate information, articles about the comings and goings of locals and editorials extolling the opportunities in the Canadian West. He was more keen on commenting on social issues of the day, creating fictional characters and passing off their antics as "real" to the shock and amazement of the Wetaskiwin community. Edwards' prose was much more personal and colourful than anything being published at the time. When he moved the *Free Lance* out of the livery stable into a former butcher shop, he made note of it in typical Bob Edwards fashion.

> *We take this opportunity of announcing that the beautiful painting of a bull's head over our new office does not signify that it is still a meat market. It was once, but not now. People wandering through our portals in search of pork chops will have to go empty away. Our patience is well nigh exhausted by children coming in and rapping on the counter with a dime, while we are dashing off an editorial on C.P.R. atrocities, and calling for ten cents worth of liver.*
>
> *—Wetaskiwin Free Lance,* May 6, 1898

It was also in Wetaskiwin that Edwards developed what would become his trademarked style: the creation of fictional characters, situations and stories to comment on social conditions, to ridicule the establishment and to tease local residents. His prose garnered him fans and enemies across the province, but it was simple finances (or rather the lack thereof) that caused Edwards to leave Wetaskiwin and sell the *Free Lance* to interests in Innisfail.

Edwards moved to Winnipeg but only for a year. He returned to Alberta, to High River, where on March 4, 1902, he founded the *Eye Opener*.

> *In the quiet cove of High River we anchor the* EYE OPENER, *hoping that I won't bust like the Maine. Clothed in righteousness, a bland smile and a lovely jag, the editor struck town two weeks ago. The management has decided on the name* "EYE OPENER" *because few people will resist it. It will run on a strictly moral basis of one dollar a year. If an immoral paper is the local preference, we can supply that too but it will cost $1.50.*

> –*Eye Opener*, March 4, 1902

As with the *Wetaskiwin Free Lance*, Edwards' style gained him both friends and enemies. But again, financial success eluded Edwards, and he decided that it made more sense to publish a paper like the *Eye Opener* in a more burgeoning metropolis. So in 1906, the High River *Eye Opener* became the Calgary *Eye Opener*, and a legend was born.

Until Edwards' death in 1922, the Calgary *Eye Opener* was one of the city's most successful newspapers, selling more than 30,000 copies of each issue. The *Eye Opener* closed its doors in 1923, less than a year after the death of its founder and editor Bob Edwards.

By this time, the newspaper industry had expanded throughout Alberta. Editors like Oliver, Wood, Saunders and Edwards could be seen as early explorers of the province, mapping out an untouched wilderness in the same way Anthony Henday and David Thompson had done.

And once the path was shown, others could follow—people who would help take the western part of the North-West Territories and allow it to grow into the province of Alberta.

∼

CHAPTER FOUR

Bob Edwards' Other Legacy

THE DEMISE OF TWO OF BOB EDWARDS' first newspapers in Alberta, the *Wetaskiwin Free Lance* and the High River version of the *Eye Opener,* led, directly and indirectly, to the establishment of a number of newspapers that would serve Alberta and their readers for many decades.

After Edwards left Wetaskiwin in August 1898, he sold his printing plant and equipment to Orville and his father George Fleming, who in turn began the *Innisfail Free Lance.* The Flemings sold the paper three years later to start the *Advocate* in Red Deer. And by 1908, the *Free Lance* would be absorbed by a new paper in town, the *Innisfail Province.* The *Province* became a vibrant newspaper in the Alberta industry and is still in operation, more than 112 years after Edwards sold the *Free Lance.*

After selling the *Free Lance,* Edwards moved to High River and founded the *Eye Opener* in 1902. When he moved to Calgary in 1906, he left the door open to one of Alberta's most successful newspaper dynasties. A failed horse trader named Charles Clark stepped into the void left by the excitable Edwards. Born in Kincardine, Ontario, Clark bought the *Okotoks Review* in 1903. His first job was to organize the type, which he found in a pile in the corner, no doubt left that way in a fit of despair and disgust by the former publisher. Clark sold his interests in Okotoks to

Interior of *High River Times* building, ca. 1940s

Printing press at the *High River Times*, ca. 1957–60

Left to right: Hugh Johnston, Ralph Brinsmead and former PM Joe Clark, at 75th anniversary of the Alberta Weekly Newpapers Association,1995

Sam Hodson, a former printer at the *Calgary Herald*, and moved to High River to begin the *High River Times* in 1905. Hodson remained at Okotoks for almost 40 years, retiring in 1947 and selling the *Okotoks Review* back to Clark.

The *Times* remained under the control of Charles Clark and his family for over 60 years and became one of the most respected weekly newspapers in the industry. For three years in a row, from 1927 to 1930, the Canadian Weekly Newspapers Association named it the best newspaper in its circulation. And in 1936, the University of Oklahoma listed the paper as one of the outstanding newspapers in North America, the only Canadian paper chosen. According to *High River and the Times*, a book written by Paul Voisey and published by the University of Alberta Press in 2004, "scarcely did a year pass prior to 1966 that the *Times* did not receive an award or an honourable mention in some category, provincially or nationally.

"Under the ownership of the Clark family, the *High River Times* came to epitomize the nature of the rural weekly press—it is a model of the genre that others aspired to emulate. From its pages, one can probe the nature of the rural weekly and unravel its purpose."

The Clark family also produced one of Canada's most respected and honoured politicians, former Prime Minister Joe Clark, grandson of Charles Clark. One of Joe Clark's first paying jobs was to deliver the *Times* for his grandfather.

So while the Calgary *Eye Opener* died with its publisher and editor Bob Edwards in 1922, part of his legacy still lives on in the *Innisfail Province* and the *High River Times*.

The High River Times

When the infamous prairie publisher, Bob Edwards, closed down the *High River Eye Opener* in 1904 and moved to Calgary, the newly incorporated village of High River was left without a newspaper.

Charles Clark, who had come to Okotoks from Kincardine, Ontario, that same year to start the *Okotoks Review*, saw an opportunity to establish a paper in High River, which was a larger centre. The first issue of the *High River Times* rolled off the press on December 5, 1905.

In those early days of printing, each letter was handpicked from a drawer of type to form a line, then line upon line was added until a page was completed. After the paper was printed, the lines were taken apart and returned, letter-by-letter, to the drawer for use the following week. The press was capable of printing only one page at a time. The ink was applied to the type, by hand, using a rubber roller. The sheet of newsprint was then laid carefully onto the type and the press was lowered on top of the paper, the pressure being applied by a long lever. Coal stoves were used to heat the building, and in mid-winter it was sometimes noon before the press was warm enough to operate.

During its early years, the *Times* was modestly successful. High River was in the midst of a land boom as settlers flooded into the area to establish homesteads. The town experienced steady commercial growth, and in that economic climate, the newspaper became well established.

The weekly edition usually consisted of eight broadsheet pages—considerably larger than the tabloid pages of today's *Times*. Only four of these pages were printed locally. The other four were general interest news and advertising printed at a plant in Regina that distributed identical pages to papers throughout the prairies.

High River Times building, ca. 1928–29

The *Times* prospered during the post-war boom days of the 1920s, and in 1927, construction of new premises took place. The one-and-a-half-storey brick structure became a High River landmark because of its prominent location and unique architecture. The cornerstone of the building was laid by John King, then president of the British Newspaper Society whose members were touring Canada at that time.

By then, a three-magazine intertype typesetting machine had replaced the tedious hand-setting method. This machinery enabled the paper to greatly increase its news and advertising content. That same year, Mrs. H.D. McCorquodale was hired as a news reporter. Some years later she became associate editor and served the paper well in that capacity until the late 1950s. During her tenure, the *Times* received recognition, nationally and provincially, for journalistic excellence.

In 1933–34, Charles Clark served as president of the Canadian Weekly Newspapers Association. Upon his death in 1949, he was succeeded as publisher by his son Charles A. Clark.

Charles Jr. had been active with the newspaper since 1929

Charles A Clark, owner of *High River Times*, ca. 1940–45

when he joined the staff as a reporter. He was fascinated by a printing process being developed at that time known as photo offset. The process involved photographing a page, or printed form, to acquire a plastic negative from which a press plate could be made.

In 1961, the miracle of photo offset came to the *Times* and with it the ability to use photo composition in advertising make-up and page design. Photographs no longer had to be sent to Calgary to have engravings made, nor was it necessary to handle molten lead to cast prepared ads and artwork. Today, virtually all newspapers are printed by the offset method, but back in 1961, the *Times* was one of the first in the province, daily or weekly.

Don Tanner joined the staff as plant foreman in 1960 and purchased the newspaper from Clark in 1966. Don learned the trade at Moosomin, Saskatchewan, and

Laying of cornerstone of the new *High River Times* office, undated

came to Alberta in 1955 to work at the *Olds Gazette*. He returned to Saskatchewan to publish the *Esterhazy Miner* at the tender age of 20 before returning to Alberta.

Under Tanner's tenure as publisher of the *Times*, the paper entered the computer age. With the acquisition of a Compugraphic 1 photo-type-setter, the intertype, which had served the paper for well over 60 years, became obsolete. Again, the *Times* was one of the first papers in Alberta to use the electronic typesetting method.

Don was a director on the national board when the federation of the provincial organizations took place and the Canadian Community Newspapers Association was formed.

In March 1978, Don sold his publishing company to Bill Holmes and Glenn Tanner. Bill had begun his career as a printer's devil in 1955 and became general manager in 1974. Glenn had been the production manager of the newspaper and commercial printing department from 1968 to 1974. The new owners constructed the building where the current newspaper office is housed. It was officially opened in May 1979 by the Right Honourable

Joe Clark—the grandson of the paper's founder.

George Meyer purchased Glenn Tanner's share of the newspaper in 1985. George, a past-president and life member of the Alberta Weekly Newspapers Association, had been involved with many Alberta weeklies, including the *Nanton News, Camrose Canadian, Taber Times* (and its subsidiary publications) and the *Claresholm Local Press*. During Meyer's tenure at High River, the Regional was instituted as a common section in partnership with the *Times* and four other weeklies in the area.

The *Times* was sold in 1995 to Westmount Press of Cochrane. Luke Vorsterman succeeded Bill Holmes as the publisher. When Bowes Publishers Ltd. bought Westmount Press in 1998, the *Times* became part of that organization with Greg Foster as publisher. He was succeeded in 2004 by current publisher Nancy Middleton.

In December 2006, the *High River Times* celebrated its 100th year.

～

CHAPTER FIVE

Provincial Expansion

O N SEPTEMBER 1, 1905, ALBERTA CEASED to be a part of the North-West Territories and was named a province of the Dominion on Canada. Considering the significance of the event, editorial comment in Alberta community newspapers was relatively muted. The reaction from most newspapers in the province was to change the "North-West Territories" on their masthead to "Alberta," although a few newspapers either let this technicality slide for several issues or simply forgot to make the modification.

There is also a good possibility that these newspapers just didn't have enough type to make the change on the exact date Alberta became a province. It's not that the weeklies were ignorant about Alberta's new status, but they may have realized that in the end, it didn't really affect or alter the day-to-day lives of Albertans of the time. Still, there were a few editorial comments.

> *This is the last issue of the News which will ever be published in the North West Territories. In the future it will be published in the Province of Alberta.*
>
> *–Nanton News*, August 31, 1905

Before our next issue reaches our readers, Alberta shall have become a Province. This change of position for which we have patiently waited has come not so soon as to be regarded lightly, and not so late as to be overestimated. In the daily life of our citizens, it will make little immediate difference. Only on occasion when the electors shall be called upon to give their judgment upon questions formerly settled for us by the Dominion Parliament, but which we shall henceforth have competence to settle for ourselves, shall the meaning and responsibility of our new position be fully disclosed.

A disinterested electorate must yield a disinterested government, and conversely, so long as electors continue to prostitute the franchise, so long will there be representatives who will serve according to the debased value of the votes by which they have been returned to power. Some appear to think a few dollars represent the value of the vote; others that some paltry office, under the government, which they or theirs shall hold uneasily for a few years, is a sufficient price; others deem a municipal advantage an equivalent and others hold the success of their party as more than enough return for their franchise. None of these holds his vote at its true value, and he who gives his vote, receiving or hoping to receive any of these things in return simply allows himself to be bribed, and becomes a traitor to his country.

–*Rocky Mountain Echo*, Pincher Creek, August 29, 1905

Reaction would come later, especially when Prime Minister Wilfrid Laurier named Edmonton as the official capital of Alberta in 1906. Although Calgary's population was larger and had more direct connections to the rest of Canada because of the CP Railway, the city and its institutions supported the losing Conservative party in the previous federal election. Edmonton, on the other hand, supported the winning Liberal party, with *Bulletin* editor Frank Oliver being named a minister in Laurier's cabinet. His connection to the prime minister offered more weight in the choice of a capital than Calgary's.

In Edmonton and in the northern part of the province, Oliver was hailed as a hero. In Calgary and southern areas, some accused him of gerrymandering in order to make Edmonton the political power holder in the province.

> *Of course, the main object in view, both with the Hon. Mr. Oliver and Mr. Talbot of Strathcona, who are the men respon-sible, was the securing of the capital for Edmonton. This they have done, regardless of any claims that Calgary has, both of conveniences and prosperity. Calgary is not a Liberal constitu-ency, unfortunately for it, and therefore has not the only claim to the capital that Mr. Oliver and Sir Wilfrid Laurier can rec-ognize. Therefore Edmonton was made the provincial seat of government. But it was feared that if a proper and fair distri-bution of seats were made in the Province, the first Assembly or Legislature might make Calgary the capital, hence the ger-rymander. And a more glaring gerrymander was never made, which it is considered that Edmonton with 6,000 people had one member, as has Calgary, with 12,000 only one also.*
>
> –*Rocky Mountain Echo*, May 16, 1906

Despite the north-south spilt, and their political differences, Alberta newspapers were as one in support of their fledging industry.

Even before Alberta became a province, newspapers in the province banded together to form an association. Spurred on by G.C. Porter, the news editor of the *Calgary Herald*, several publishers from Alberta and eastern BC met in Calgary for two days in August 1904. They formed the Alberta and Eastern British Columbia Press Association. During the convention, they drafted a constitution and heard a speech on the *Law of Libel as it Applies to Editors and Publishers* that later became the basis for the development of Alberta's first Libel Law.

Newspaper office of *Castor Advance*, 1911

The newspaper industry expanded throughout Alberta during the late 19th century and into the early years of the 20th. As more towns and villages became established, more and more newspapers were created. From Ponoka to Pincher Creek, Carstairs to Castor, Raymond to Ryley, local newspapers came into being. From 1890 to 1905, over 90 weekly newspapers were founded throughout Alberta, several of them even before their respective towns, hamlets or villages were recognized as official settlements. A few of these publications, such as the *Ponoka Herald,* the *Olds Gazette* and the *Lloydminster Times,* managed to last almost a century. The *Ponoka Herald* ceased operations in 1997; the *Olds Gazette* was sold to Great West Publishing in 2005 and absorbed into that chain, while the *Lloydminster Times,* until its closure in 2000, was the longest running business in that town. Two of the newspapers to open during this period, the *Lacombe Globe* and the *Pincher Creek Echo,* are still in business today.

Left to right: W.F. Beamish, G.C. Duncan and Frank Whiteside, editor of the *Castor Advance*, 1909

From 1905 to 1914, the beginning of World War I, 191 weekly newspapers were founded in Alberta, including many still operating today, such as the *Leduc Representative*, the *Stettler Independent*, the *Vegreville Observer*, the *Sedgewick Sentinel* (now called the *Sedgewick Community Press*), the *Castor Advance*, the *Strathmore Standard*, the *Vermilion Standard*, the *Brooks Bulletin*, the *Coronation Review*, the *Taber Times*, the *Consort Enterprise*, the *Hanna Herald*, the *Vulcan Advocate* and the *Three Hills Capital*.

"Where did our early newspapermen come from as issue number one, volume number one, appeared in one prairie town after another?" wrote Leonard D'Albertanson, publisher of the *Wainwright Star* and editor of *The Printed Word: The Story of the Alberta Division of the Canadian*

Weekly Newspapers Association, published in 1955. "Their sources were legion. From Saskatchewan and Manitoba, from Ontario, from the Maritimes, the Old Country, from the United States, came young men, many with wives and families, many after an unsatisfactory interlude in tilling the virgin sod and many with very little experience and less capital. Pioneers in spirit…frontiersmen among frontiersmen…a lot as varied in talent as in appearances, but possessing those sterling and essential qualities…perseverance and determination."

Many of these early newspapers folded within a year or two for reasons numerous and varied. Others were lucky to make it through a decade of operation. No doubt the opportunities for generating income in a town or village with a population less than 300 was limited.

> *The numerous reports and editorials these days on the financial stringency is sure proof that every newspaper is up against it. There are several reasons why it could not be other wise. To begin with, a very large majority of our Alberta towns, where newspapers exist, are altogether too small to warrant the establishing of the paper. The petty jealousies between neighbouring towns makes it impossible for one paper to serve a reasonable district because business men will not give patronage to a paper published anywhere except in their own hamlet. They will leave no stone unturned to get a paper of their own started and want the best brains and equipment in the land, but when a money stringency arise the editor and printer is one of the first to suffer. Advertising is curtailed or cut out altogether, soap wrappers or something as cheap is substituted for properly printed stationary and it becomes almost impossible for the publisher to collect enough to pay the actually running expenses. And yet, what agency has done more to build up the town and assist its business men to success.*
>
> *–Claresholm Review, August 28, 1913*

Unfortunately, less than one year after this editorial appeared in the *Claresholm Review*, a rival paper, the *Claresholm Advertiser*, opened. Although Claresholm was an Alberta town that could support one newspaper, in no way could it support two for long, especially during the recession that raged in Alberta at that time. The publisher of the *Advertiser*, Harwood Duncan, was aware of this situation since he had been publisher of the *Review* when that editorial ran.

For reasons unknown, L.G. "Shorty" Shortreed became the owner of the *Review* in January 1914, but Duncan didn't wait long to launch a competing paper. The *Advertiser* began in March 1914, and two years later, after Shortreed moved to Toronto, Duncan bought the plant and the business interests of the *Review*. On Friday, April 7, 1916, the *Claresholm Review-Advertiser* was launched. The situation repeated itself in 1928 when the *Review-Advertiser* was absorbed by the *Claresholm Local Press*, another local rival.

Over the decades, the *Local Press* went through a series of owners and as of 2012, is still independently owned and operated on the same lot where it started, albeit in a new building. Roxanne Thompson is the current owner and publisher of the *Local Press*, having purchased the paper in July 2005.

A good number of publishers/editors of early Alberta newspapers were keen writers, advertising sales people and community-minded, but they were inexperienced in the practical and time-consuming aspects of producing a newspaper week after week, especially in a time when most of the type in the newspaper had to be handset.

Before the development and widespread use of Linotype and offset presses, just getting the paper designed and printed was an arduous process. Many publishers used hand presses, such as the famous Washington hand press, to produce their weekly publication.

Woman using a Washington hand press, 1939

"Whatever type face was available, or available at the right price, forthwith became the dress of the newspaper," wrote noted newspaper designer Edmund C. Arnold in 1961.

> *Type was so small the printer could lug it to some outpost with a minimum of effort. Even that minimum was far beyond the sweat today's newspapermen must expend, for enough 6-point type to set a small 4-page paper weighed heavily upon the back when it was toted over the faint wagon ruts that led westward. Pictures were practically non-existent. If the printer/editor was unusually deft and had the time, he might carve a wood engraving. If he was so fortunate as to come upon a metal engraving, he cherished it as he would his wife.*

Many publishers relied on boilerplate or ready-to-print material, which in the early days were typically pages of type, set and locked in place

William Bleasdell Cameron, 1947

~

so they could easily be used as pages in a paper or dropped in any hole in a page. Most boilerplate featured a wide variety of articles—news of the world, jokes, agricultural advice, serialized novels and "information" articles about the "wretchedness of constipation" or "exhausted brains and nervous systems," which in truth were blatant ads hawking snake-oil remedies with names like Doctor Chase's Nerve Tonic or Minaurd's Neuralgia Liniment.

Few editors liked boilerplate because the local character of a newspaper was deemed significant in its appeal to readers—some news was old by the time it appeared and was usually set in a different type style than other news. But boilerplate was seen as a financial necessity; few papers could succeed without it.

The *Fort Macleod Gazette* banned boilerplate from its pages in 1910, but that experiment didn't last. Within months, financial insecurity brought boilerplate back into the folds of the paper. Boilerplate remained a mainstay of newspapers in the early days of the industry, but by the 1920s, most of it had disappeared, replaced by syndicated news, which functioned in the same manner of boilerplate but at least it could be set in the same type face and style as the rest of the newspaper.

But even with the wide availability of boilerplate, many pages in a local newspaper still had to be handset and then printed using human power alone.

"I was elected to run the plant and after six months of hand-setting news and ads, and operating a Washington hand press, I secretly wished that Cameron hadn't survived the [Frog Lake] massacre," Leonard Nesbitt wrote in *The Printed Word*. Nesbitt was an early pioneer in the Alberta weekly newspaper industry. He and his partner, James Sharp, had been reporters for the *Calgary Herald* and bought the *Bassano News* in 1912 from William Cameron, a noted journalist and also the only male survivor of the 1885 Frog Lake Massacre (see Frog Lake Survivor, p. 49).

Nesbitt later bought the *Brooks Bulletin*, which his descendants still publish.

"In those early days the production of the newspaper was a laborious and painfully slow process. Everything was handset and the distribution of the type took a lot of time. Gasoline engines provided the motive power for the presses but in many instances foot power was used for the platen," Nesbitt further wrote in *The Printed Word*. "The Diamond newspaper press could be operated manually. It is related of one weekly publisher who had a platen without a throw-off and when he wanted to stop the press suddenly, he would grab the fly-wheel and go around it with a couple of times."

"One of the features which complicated the printing business for the pioneer was the fact that his machinery, at least his heavy machinery,

The late Jim Nesbitt (centre), publisher of the *Brooks Bulletin*, with sons Jon (left) and Jamie, 2003

was at least secondhand, and very often had seen service on many fronts before it found its place in his humble shop," wrote Leonard D'Albertanson. "In its peregrinations it had generally lost a few parts, reached a fairly advanced stage of decay, and developed peculiarities and eccentricities which on occasion overshadowed those of its harassed owner. While the movie versions of the country print shop may be somewhat imaginative, there is every reason to believe that the average editor's mechanical ability and patience developed and blossomed profusely (as did his vocabulary) as he coaxed his weekly product through a rather shaky production line."

Frog Lake Survivor

One of the individuals to found a small weekly newspaper in the early part of the 20th century in Alberta was William Bleasdell Cameron. On March 1, 1906, he began the *Vermilion Signal*. Although Cameron had already amassed years of journalism experience before founding the *Signal*—including a stint as editor of the venerable *Field and Stream* in New York—he had already found a place in Canadian history.

Born in Trenton, Ontario, in 1862, Cameron apprenticed as a pharmacist but a quest for adventure drew him west. After working at various jobs throughout the years, he took a job as a Hudson's Bay Company trader in Frog Lake, a small settlement just west of the present Alberta-Saskatchewan border. He had a respectful relationship with the local Cree band, headed by the legendary Chief Big Bear, and they gave him the name, N-Chawamis, or My Little Brother.

Fortunately for Cameron, his relationship with the Cree may have saved his life. Angered by unfair treaties, the disappearance of the buffalo (their main source of food) and possibly emboldened by Louis Riel's North-West Rebellion in Manitoba, several Cree warriors took over the Frog Lake settlement on April 2, 1885. By the end of the day, nine white men were killed.

"High over all swelled the deadly war chant of the Plain Crees, bursting from a hundred sinewy throats. I heard Wandering Spirit shout to his followers to shoot the whites and crack after crack told of the deaths of other of my friends," Cameron wrote in his 1927 book, *Blood Red the Sun*. "My first thought was to seize an axe, lock myself in the house and brain the first man to force the door. But I looked about and could see no axe. An Indian raced up to me, holding his gun before him. 'If you speak twice, you are a dead man,' he cried."

With the help of some of the warriors not involved in the massacre, Cameron made his way to a Cree encampment, where several Native women hid him under a shawl. He was the only male

Horse Child (left), son of Chief Big Bear, with William Bleasdell Cameron. They were photographed together in 1885 during the trial of Big Bear. Cameron testified in Big Bear's defence.

∼

survivor of what is known in Canadian history as the Frog Lake Massacre.

Cameron edited the *Vermilion Signal* until 1910 before moving south to found the *Bassano News*. He sold that newspaper within a year to Leonard Nesbitt, whose grandsons still publish the *Brooks Bulletin*.

William Bleasdell Cameron moved from one business venture after another before passing away on March 4, 1951, in Meadow Lake, less than 150 kilometres east of Frog Lake.

∼

BROOKS BULLETIN

The land surrounding the city of Brooks was the home and the hunting ground of the Blood and Blackfoot Indians before Treaty No. 7 was signed at the Blackfoot Crossing on the Bow River near Gleichen on September 22, 1877. The treaty and the arrival of the North West Mounted Police meant that a large tract of semi-arid land with nutritious prairie grass was made available to incoming ranchers. In 1881 the Dominion Government set regulations that permitted a rancher to lease areas up to 100,000 acres for an annual rental of one cent per acre.

The land around Brooks was surveyed in 1882, and the following year the CPR pushed its transcontinental line from Medicine Hat to Brooks and westward to Calgary where it arrived on August 11, 1883. By the time the railway was completed, the buffalo had almost disappeared and ranchers were moving in. One rancher, George Lane, had 24,000 cattle on his lease in 1906. It was Lane who recommended Brooks' first citizen, Ernest Morden Crooker, for the appointment for district government brand inspector.

A native of Ontario, Crooker worked on ranches in southern Alberta but gave up ranch work in 1904, when he and his wife built a store close to the stockyards that the railway had constructed for the convenience of the ranchers. There was no Brooks at that time; it was just a flag stop at mile 723 west of Winnipeg. The Crookers provided meals and beds for the cowboys when they delivered cattle for shipment; the family's livery barn and combined hotel, café and grocery store laid the foundation for the present city of Brooks.

The townsite was surveyed in 1907, by which time the population was nine: five railway employees, Mr. and Mrs. Jim Pierce and the Crookers. Shortly after 1907, the CPR started to construct a dam across the Bow

Brothers Howard (left) and Leonard Nesbitt preparing to put up sign for the *Brooks Bulletin* building, April 1912

~

River at Bassano and irrigated a tract of their huge holdings adjacent to the railway. The dam was completed in 1914, which signified the start of irrigation in the 2340-square-mile block—an area larger than the province of Prince Edward Island.

By 1910 the population of the town was growing as business interests established grocery and hardware stores, lumber yards and rooming houses.

The residents incorporated the hamlet as a village, named after CPR employee Noel Edgel

Brooks. Businessmen wanted to attract the business of the homesteaders so they formed a Board of Trade and elected E.O. (Bert) Coultis as editor to start up a newspaper that he named the *Brooks Bulletin* for circulation throughout the area. Coultis solicited advertising, wrote general news items and then had the paper printed in Medicine Hat.

In the fall of 1910, a man named Calvin Goss came to Brooks with the intention to start a newspaper; his arrival was welcomed by Coultis, whose principal job

Brothers Leonard (left) and Howard Nesbitt inside the *Brooks Bulletin* office, April 1912

was to operate the Bowman-Sine Lumber Company.

Goss produced a four-page newspaper called *The Banner* that was made using hand type—each letter was picked out of a case by hand. He ran the paper for a year and a half, then sold it to Leonard D. Nesbitt for $500. The name of the paper was changed from *The Banner* back to the *Brooks Bulletin*.

About four days were devoted to publishing the newspaper and two days to commercial printing. Homesteaders often lost their horses, which provided business for the printer at a rate of $2 for 100 small handbills that described the horse and brands if any. Rents were comparatively cheap; a small building 16 by 24 feet cost $10 a month—it was the whole printing plant.

World War I caused a slump in the town's economy because several men left to fight, and the work on the irrigation project ceased. Toward the end of the war, times got better. The railway brought in extra personnel to expand the operation of the irrigation district, and settlers moved in to take up the irrigated land.

The editor and one printer managed to publish the *Bulletin* with the help of a printer's devil. Thus, the staff at the *Bulletin* remained fairly constant until after World War II. Labour-saving machines such as the Linotype, which set type in blocks of hot lead, and semi-automatic presses took up the slack.

It was customary for community papers at that time to appoint a correspondent—usually a farmer's wife—to write about the small happenings and the comings and goings of the residents in each community.

Over the years, a few members of the Nesbitt family, including Leonard's brother Howard and sons Clive and Lee, edited and published the *Bulletin* until 1954 when Leonard's youngest son, Jim, became publisher. He semi-retired in 1982 but continued to write editorials and a column. Jim passed away in November 2005. Today, Leonard Nesbitt's grandsons Jamie and Jon oversee the day-to-day operations of the paper.

The *Bulletin* occupies a modern 10,000-square-foot building in downtown Brooks with 12 full-time and 10 part-time employees. Along with a news-gathering staff of three, there are 20 country correspondents and several contributing columnists through syndication services. The paper is published every Tuesday regardless of holidays and enjoys a circulation of some 4000 newspapers delivered through the mail and sold over counters throughout the district.

Office and production areas are fully computerized with separate systems handling the invoicing, subscription and payroll records and all typesetting for newspaper and commercial printing production.

The paper is printed on a seven-unit Goss Community newspaper press that can print a 16-page section at speeds close to 15,000 sections per hour. The paper averages 42 broadsheet pages each week, making it one of the largest weekly papers in the country.

The *Bulletin* uses close to 80 metric tonnes of newsprint and up to 250 gallons of ink per year. Newsprint arrives in 20-tonne shipments from mills in northern Alberta and is stored on the premises.

The *Bulletin* is a member of the AWNA along with over 100 other papers in Alberta and also the Canadian Community Newspaper Association, which has a membership across the country of a little more than 600 papers.

The paper follows the policy of all weekly papers in that it concentrates on local events, no matter how insignificant they may seem to an outsider. Community newspapers over the years have acquired the reputation of specializing in publishing the names of people and the life events that surround them, from births to school accomplishments to wedding write-ups and other facets of the social life of the community as well as obituaries. Over the years, the *Bulletin* decided to add columns on special items of interest.

The paper strives to make readers think for themselves and take a vested interest in local happenings whether or not they agree with the subject matter. The *Bulletin* acts as a watchdog of sorts by ensuring residents are aware of the various events and changes that affect their everyday lives.

∼

Despite the troubles with machinery, some newspapers did last longer, maybe another decade, but the recession prior to World War I knocked the province for a loop and took many newspapers with it. A few continued on with the original owner but then many papers died soon after the death of their founders. But a good number of newspapers that started in the first 15 or 20 years of the 20th century thrived and prospered. Some newspapers passed from one publisher to the next and either folded at some point or found the right combination of owner, timing, location and editorial style in order to succeed. Many also passed from one generation to the next and became integral parts of the community they served.

"Like any other business, newspapers existed to make money for their owners. But they were a special type of business," wrote Donald

Wetherell in the *Town Life: Main Street and the Evolution of Small Town Alberta, 1880–1947*, published by the University of Alberta Press in 1995. "Like city newspapers, they served an important and unique function in promoting the town and providing news, commentary and entertainment. Although these broad functions were inseparable, emphasis on a particular function varied with each paper's editor. The centrality of town promotion and the need for advertising created a certain uniformity in the nature of town newspapers. Yet many had an individuality that stemmed from the characters of their editors. Their pet concerns and projects made their way into the papers in editorials or news reports or in special features. While there was a high turnover in the business, many editors had remarkable staying power."

> *Our object at present is to give our readers a bright and newsy weekly which will enable them to keep more in touch with everyday and happenings in the country. It is essentially a local paper we will bend all over our energies towards the advancement of High River and her people. In politics, it is our purpose to pursue a strictly non-partisan course. We realize that we are receiving support of persons from varying political opinions and that their interests are ours and we intend to remain free to praise the good and upbraid the evil wherever in our humble opinion either may appear. Still we feel that where their is only one paper in a town it should keep itself as nearly as possible not influenced by party politics: with us it is High River first, last and always. However, without the support of the people we can do very little and therefore sincerely trust that those who have already give us their support will continue to do so in the interest of the community and assist accordingly.*
>
> *–High River Times*, December 6, 1905

By 1920, Alberta had 100 newspapers, 94 of them being weekly newspapers. In that same year, the weeklies struck out on their own. The Canadian Press Association, which had originally included all types of newspapers in its organizations, split the dailies and weeklies into two separate organizations. Nationally, weeklies formed the Canadian Weekly Newspapers Association, and in Alberta, they formed the Alberta Weekly Newspapers Association (AWNA).

But before the umbrella organizations were created, Alberta suffered through a series of tribulations that tested the mettle of its citizens, including a severe recession, an influenza epidemic and a global conflict that became known as the Great War.

CHAPTER SIX

The Great War

THE ASSASSINATION OF AUSTRIAN archduke Franz Ferdinand on June 28, 1914, reached deep into the heart of Alberta.

The front page of the August 5, 1914, edition of the *Claresholm Advertiser* said it all:

BRITAIN IS AT WAR:

Canada will do her part.

Throughout Alberta, newspapers had similar heads, stories outlining the situation in Europe and articles noting support of King and Country against the Kaiser and what war would mean to the local area.

> *The serious conditions arising from the European war situation do not confine themselves to any country or class of people, but will reach all, in varying measure. They will, undoubtedly, be brought home to the people of Banff and Western Canada generally in the tightening of finances, which again, is inevitable.*
>
> *The banks have already withdrawn support in the way of advances to merchandise, both wholesale and retail. It will follow, unquestionably that the small merchant must confine his sales to cash which will work unavoidable hardship on many. The wise course for everyone will be to confine their*

purchases to necessities and avoid assuming unnecessary obligations.

One need not be alarmist to realize that the financial situation is a serious one. Should the war be only of short duration, it will take months for the different countries affected to resume approximate normal footing. Meanwhile, patriotism can be expressed in tangible measure by everyone willing to do their share in facing the problems and difficulties which the crisis brings.

–Banff Crag and Canyon, August 8, 1914

Despite the realistic tone of Norman K. Luxton's editorial, not many were prepared for the depth of tragedy to come. Most expected the war to last only a few months, a year at most. Many newspapers encouraged the enlistment of locals, sometimes directly, sometimes not, in articles celebrating the victories won by the Allies, bittersweet description of boys leaving town on the local train to serve or descriptions of loyalty by area residents.

The present war which is the largest that this world has ever known of has caused Great Britain to send to this colony for assistants. This assistance was first answered by Alberta who asked for men from all over the province. As soon as the call came, thousands of young men willingly offered their services. Six of this number were asked to volunteer from Claresholm and the call was answered in a very short time by some twenty young men who are willing to sacrifice their lives for the protection of the power which Great Britain now has.

Saturday night many of the citizens gathered in the I.O.O.F. hall to give the boys a farewell supper and formal sendoff to the front. Sunday morning when the flier pulled into the station, over three hundred were there to say goodbye and hoped it was not goodbye forever.

–Claresholm Review, August 13, 1914

Some person or other has brought back a story to Wainwright about "Scotty" the formerly porter at the Wainwright hotel and the run of it is of this fashion: Scotty, after a send off at the Wainwright depot and enjoyable ride to the capital, arrived at the recruiting offices of the infantry battalion now being raised. He stood his place in line and accordingly stripped to the waist for medical inspection. His chest was fine as were many parts of his anatomy but his teeth brought an exclamation from the offices that they would never do. Scotty, momentarily stunned by such a remark and looking up, said, "What do ye think I want to do the Germans, eat them?" The result was that the officer sent Scotty across to the dentist who fixed the defective molars. Scotty is now a full-fledged soldier of the king.

—Wainwright Star, January 20, 1915

Young men of Lethbridge, your duty is clear. Your country calls. Canada calls. It is not the Motherland alone who needs you. The Dominion needs you. Are you content to stay at home and pass your hours in business and in pleasure in between the hours, when every able-bodied man is wanted on the firing line to save the Empire from a future which, however impossible it may seem, may become a possibility if you fail in your duty.

We have during the campaign just closed heard a great deal of being a man. That opportunity has been open to the young men of this city since August 4th. It is an opportunity which needed no arguments to justify its seizure by every young man physically fit. And yet, there are young men in Lethbridge and in the country around who have turned a deaf ear to a call which requires no argument to justify it.

Many have already done their individual duty by enlisting. But there are others, who have not. There are young men

physically fit with no particular ties, in the city today whose
place should be on the fire line or who should be preparing
themselves with others for getting there for their country's
need, and their country urgently needs them.

–Lethbridge Telegraph, July 22, 1915

Possibly in response to these articles, thousands of Albertans enlisted. By the end of the war, 48,885 Albertans would enlist, almost four percent of the province's population, more than twice the national average. In Gleichen, 250 men in the small village signed up. In Ashmont, 15 men enlisted at the same time. In Frank, Alberta, Anne Dunlop's husband and their three sons enlisted within of six months of each other in 1915. In every town, in every community, fathers, husband, sons, brothers, sweethearts—many from the same family—signed up to serve King and Country.

A number of Alberta newspapermen also put aside their journalistic ambitions and enlisted. The editor of the *Okotoks Observer*, Henry Arthur Harding, had many years of experience in the militia, even holding a captain's certificate, but he chose to enlist as a regular soldier. His father had been the editor of the *Port Rowan News* in Ontario since 1893, and Henry first wound up in Okotoks in 1911 as the sub-editor of the *Okotoks Advance*.

After the *Advance* folded in 1913, Harding worked as a journalist in Calgary, only to return to Okotoks in the spring of 1914, this time as the publisher and editor of the *Okotoks Observer*. It was a solid newspaper that was not only readable in a content sense but also stylistic. The *Observer*'s leading was larger than what other newspapers of the time used, and Harding used little boilerplate, focusing instead on local news that wouldn't be out of place in a current weekly, and not just comings and goings of area residents. Photographs were also a regular feature, and almost all of the advertising came from local businesses.

For some unknown reason, Harding usually signed his editorials "Wamba," possibly a reference to a seventh-century Spanish king. Once war was declared, he put the newspaper business behind him.

The EDITOR of THE OBSERVER *has converted his trusty fountain pen into a rifle and has departed for the front where it is his intention to do great execution among the Germans and Austrians. Tis sad that it must be so; but so it is and it cannot be helped. General Sherman once said that, "War is Hell!" The Editor is convinced that beside the job of running a small newspaper in a small town, it will prove to be an affair of peace and quietness.*

Moratura Vos Salutamas!
WAMBA

–*Okotoks Observer*, August 13, 1914.

Homer S. Mohr took over the editorial duties of the *Observer*, but the paper folded less than two weeks after Harding's final editorial.

William Fraser "Mac" McAllister, a reporter for the *Medicine Hat News*, signed up barely four days after Harding. Norman Cook, a former teacher who had purchased the *Wainwright Star* from H. Cummer in 1912, signed up on February 11, 1915, listing Newspaper Publisher as his trade, or calling, on the enlistment application (see Dispatches from the Front, p. 71).

Cook's replacement in Wainwright, W.H. Webb, edited the *Star* for only another year; he was on the frontlines in France by April 1916. Other staff at the newspaper also signed up—pressmen, printer's devils, reporters, labourers and contributors.

Arthur Elmer Bates was a Holborn-area homesteader who contributed poetry and letters to several early Alberta weeklies under the title of "Hobo Bard." For a few months he published the *Irma Imp*, using a printing press that he ran on his homestead, but he also enlisted in 1915.

During the first couple years of the war, the Alberta and BC Division of the Canadian Press Association held no conventions or any major meetings. In 1916, a convention was held in Calgary on August 24 and 25 with two main topics of discussion. First, publishers were concerned about the free advertising space they were giving to patriotic organizations. The publishers had no qualms about doing their part by offering the free advertising, but in the words of Bob Jennings of the *Edmonton Journal,* "charitable and patriotic organizations were accustomed to consider gratis newspaper advertising as not even worthy of thanks. By insisting that credit be given in such cases the organization which is recipient will more fully realize what the newspapers are giving." So a resolution was passed asking that such organizations give credit on their books for free publicity at the prevailing advertising rates.

The other resolution passed at the convention was more historic to the Alberta newspaper industry. Since there were more newspapers on both sides of the continental divide, it was decided that each province would strike out on its own. In August 1916, the Alberta Division of the Canadian Press was first established.

In the first 18 months of the war, most of the news presented in Alberta papers focused on the big picture of the war, of various battles fought by European allies, and little about Canadian soldiers. Only as Canadians became more involved in the war, participating in such key battles as the Somme, Ypres and Passchendaele, did the news change.

Many newspapers ran letters from soldiers that were submitted by their families. Some papers had a weekly column updating the status of every local soldier who had enlisted, including such information as promotions or postings to various locales. But every so often, the news was not good.

Almost every week, in almost every newspaper, a note would state that a local boy had been wounded in action, what hospital he was in, his condition and whether he would be sent home or back to the front. In a few odd cases, corrections had to be made.

> *Dear Sir—Having read the article in your paper headed "Two local boys were wounded" in which the writer, Pte. Billy Reid figures as one of the wounded, I would like to state that there is absolutely no truth in the report. I do not know how this information could have got around. All I sent was a field service post card to Mr. J.M. Morrison which stated: "I am quite well. I am in the best of health and since I have been on this side of the herring pond," and as the article in question has probably given my many friends in the Hat just cause for anxiety, I would ask you to kindly contradict same in the columns of your paper.*
>
> *Yours truly,*
> *Pte. Billy Reid*
> *3rd CMR*
>
> *PS: Everything is jake with the lever up.*
>
> *–Medicine Hat News*, December 20, 1915

And every few weeks there was more tragic news. For example, out of the 250 Gleichen men who had enlisted, one in five never returned. Out of the 15 Ashmont men who enlisted, only five came back. All three of the Dunlop brothers from Frank, Alberta, were killed. Their father survived, and despite the deaths of his three sons, he served overseas throughout the entire war. The heartbreaking circumstances of the war hit home, one telegram at a time.

> *Three of my aunties boyfriends, two of my brothers and three uncles left so the dear ones would not be slaves. I loved my uncles and my aunties' sweethearts dearly. Little did I realize that so many would never return from that terrible battle. Then the telegrams started to arrive and I do not remember the order in which they came. How my aunts, my mother*

and my grandmother stood it, I do not know. A neighbour, William Guest, killed in action. Another neighbour, William Wood, was seriously wounded. This seemed to be just a nightmare but then it really happened. We were told that William Adkins was killed helping a wounded comrade to safety. I will never forget the card that grandmother received on Uncle Will's death. When I read that card I went up in my uncles log barn loft and cried like an orphaned child. My grannie had one son still on the battlefield but after such a tragedy to come to one mother he was moved to a safer position.

–Dick Adkins, *Westlock News, Jubilee Edition,* 1955

Almost every newspaper ran a notice or article when a local soldier was killed in action. Almost all were written in a straightforward manner, just the facts without any exclamations of grief or comments from families. The more personal stories came later, in letters from the front that family members, friends, sweethearts or colleagues gave to the local newspaper for publication.

Almost every newspaper in the province published these letters, giving the war a more homespun touch. Some deaths, though, hit the Alberta newspaper industry a bit closer. On June 6, 1916, Henry Arthur Harding, the former publisher and editor of the *Okotoks Observer* was killed by a German sniper. Although he enlisted as a private, he was later commissioned as a lieutenant.

Brother Harding was a gentleman of culture, a bachelor of arts of Trinity College, Toronto. Those who had the pleasure of personal contact with him intimately in their own home knew him as a sincere friend, an entertaining conversationalist who showed a wide knowledge of English Literature, British History and especially military history. It was his delight to describe in detail the field and events of Waterloo or some other battleground, which he seemed to be able to give at a moment's notice. He was in his element when offering his services for the war as a soldier. He has made the ultimate sacrifice, we believe, cheerfully and ungrudgingly.

–Okotoks Review, June 23, 1916

Also killed in action was Orville D. Fleming who, along with his father George, had taken over the *Wetaskiwin Free Lance* from Bob Edwards in 1898. The Flemings would also found the *Penhold Reporter* and the *Albertan Echo* but are better known for the 1901 founding of the now daily *Red Deer Advocate.* Private Orville Fleming was killed on September 7, 1917, during the Battle of Passchendaele.

Also killed in Passchendaele was Hobo Bard, aka Arthur Elmer Bates, a regular contributor to Alberta's weeklies. He died on October 30, 1917.

Along with the tragic listings of those killed or wounded in action came stories of bravery and valour. In 1916, the then weekly *Grande Prairie Herald* ran a story about a local homesteader. At the outbreak of hostilities in 1914, John Chipman "Chip" Kerr and his brother immediately left their Spirit River farm for Edmonton to enlist. On the door of the Kerrs' humble shack they left a note: "War is hell, but what is homesteading?"

The details of the daring single-handed attack upon a German trench by Private J.C. Kerr were furnished in a letter written by Colonel Griesbach:

> *Some marvelous things were done. I never saw anything like it. Kerr, of Spirit River and formerly of Edmonton's 66th Battalion, did a great piece of work. We were fighting up a trench with bombs and were running short. Kerr jumped out of the trench and ran along the edge of it and jumped the Germans single-handed, using the rifle and bayonet. The Huns thought they were cut off and sixty-two of them surrendered and gave up 250 yards of trench. Kerr had a finger blown off at the second joint but never stopped going till he and another fellow took the prisoners to the rear. Then his wound was dressed and he was ready to go on with the fight and finally had to be ordered to the rear before he would quit.*

All of those who knew "Chip" before he enlisted with the 66th are enthusiastic over his recent exploit. His action, however, does not come as a surprise. It seems to be a case of "just what I expected of him."

–*Grande Prairie Herald,* November 1, 1916

Kerr's actions garnered him the Victoria Cross, one of only three Albertans to receive the award in the Great War. He returned to Spirit River, married and raised four sons and one daughter. He later served in World War II, losing one of his sons in that war. Kerr passed away in Port Moody in 1963.

Another story of bravery came from the Sedgewick area. Private Cecil Kinross was a farmer from Lougheed who enlisted in the Canadian Overseas Expeditionary Forces on October 21, 1915. He served on many fronts, including the Passchendaele Ridge.

Young Kinross was just 19 years old when he enlisted and has been thrice wounded on the firing line: once in September 1916, and again in the spring of 1917. His third wounding came in the heroic exploit that brought him the coveted V.C. Shortly after an attack was launched, the company to which he belonged came under intense artillery fire and its further advance was held up by a very severe fire from an enemy machine gun. Private Kinross, making a very careful survey of the situation, deliberately divested himself of all his equipment save his rifle and bandolier and regardless of his personal safety, advanced alone over the open ground in broad daylight, killing the crew of six and seized and destroyed the gun. His superb example and courage instilled the greatest confidence in his company and enabled a further advance of 300 yards to be made and an important position to be established. Throughout the day he showed marvelous coolness and courage, fighting with the utmost aggressiveness and against heavy odds until severely wounded.

He is now in Orpington Hospital and progressing nicely. His wounds are in the head and arm.

–Sedgewick Sentinel, January 24, 1918

Kinross returned to Alberta and lived a colourful life in Lougheed before passing away in 1957.

When the Armistice was signed on November 11, 1918, more than 60,000 Canadians, including more than 6800 Albertans, had been killed in the war. More than 20,000 Albertans were wounded, almost half the number that had enlisted. Many newspapers had mentions or stories concerning the end of the war, save for the *Banff Crag and Canyon.* The paper had ceased production the week before the end of the war for its annual winter sabbatical and had missed one of the most important stories of the decade.

Prior to the official signing of the Armistice, an erroneous report that the war was over began in London and trickled throughout the Empire through the use of the relatively new telephone system. This early yet incorrect statement made front-page news in many Alberta newspapers.

Some explanation is due our readers with regard to the announcement in last week's paper that the Germans had made complete surrender. This was telephoned through from a Calgary newspaper office as being official, and reached us as we were about to go to press. Earlier dispatches had reported a German delegation on its way to arrange terms of armistice with Marshall Foch and it was naturally accepted as correct that the armistice had been signed. Being sent through as official, we had no hesitation in publishing the report and it was not until the edition had been printed that word came through that this announcement was premature.

That this report was widespread and dependence placed on it is evidenced by the fact that press dispatches later told of demonstrations being held in New York, Washington, Montreal,

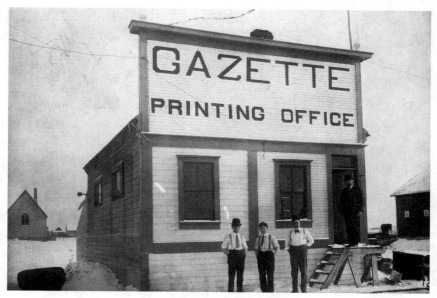

Olds Gazette building, undated

⌒

Calgary and other places. In each of these places the populace gave themselves up to celebrating the Victory.

–Olds Gazette, November 14, 1918

For the most part though, people did not dance too much in the streets of small-town Alberta. There were bonfires, speeches and impromptu dances. And later, there was some gloating and anger about how the Germans had fought the war, but mostly it was just a sigh of relief that it was finally over and that the boys who had survived would soon return home. But the war lasted years longer than anyone ever expected, laid waste to the plains of continental Europe and robbed a generation of its innocence.

We celebrate today with feelings of sorrow because of the heart-rending sacrifices which many of our fellow citizens and countrymen have nobly made, to secure our posterity that peace which this victory alone could guarantee.

To the heart-broken mothers and fathers; to the poor and lonely widows; to the fatherless children and to the fallen and maimed heroes of this great and free empire we owe a debt that cannot be repaid.

But let us thank God, as we commemorate this great day, that their sacrifices have not been made in vain; for the glorious peace which will follow this magnificent Allied victor will ever stand as a monument to their heroic and valorous deeds.

Let us then, with mingled feelings of joy and pain together give thanks and after, with unstinted energy devote ourselves to the task which is before us.

–Medicine Hat Weekly News, November 14, 1918

Dispatches from the Front

Norman Cook was the owner and editor of the *Wainwright Star* when war broke out in Europe in 1914. Although he had no military training, Cook felt it was important for him to serve King and Country by enlisting. He was 25 years old. For almost two years, Cook served as a defacto war correspondent for the *Star*, sending back letters, telegrams and dispatches about his experiences.

> *We are enjoying more comforts here than we ever expected. In the trenches we have dug-outs into which we go for spasmodic sleeps between watches. We take our blankets with us and sleep on sandbags in the dug-outs. We have fine grub—ham, steak, potatoes, bread and butter tea and sometimes coffee. When in the trenches, we do our own cooking.*
>
> *–Wainwright Star,* November 17, 1915,

Along with his dispatches, Cook (or someone else) sent a photograph of the boys from Wainwright that ran in the *Star.* In some instances, the photo was the final image of a local lad before he was killed in action.

And despite army censors checking his letters, Cook's notes were informative and honest.

> *When notified to come up for leave, we were at Hooge. The Germans up there are bad ones and tried to slip it over on us but didn't get away. We lost a good bunch of men, but other battalions suffered even more severely. One of the boys on my gun was shot accidentally and I hold myself responsible for his death seeing that it was the machine gun of which I was in charge. There is no use of me going into details in this short note, I have lots to say though.*
>
> *–Wainwright Star,* May 3, 1916

Cook's note was the last that readers of the *Star* would hear from him for more than six months. During that time, he saw more action in France, and he also sold his newspaper to C.R Morrison. On December 27, 1916, the *Wainwright Star* received its final dispatch from the now-corporal Norman Cook, a story about the local Wainwright band, headed by Art King, playing for troops in France.

As I looked down the long straight road, Lo! and behold there was Mr. King at the head of the column of this with his brass band glittering in the sun behind. When he came past he caught site of me and his face broke into a broad smile that showed he had seen something familiar. Behind him were Bert Porter, two Graingers, Frank Stott, Freddy Pawling and the other King boy and several other Wainwright boys. It did seem good to see them again and certainly made me think of home and feel proud of these newcomers. We had many a hearty laugh during the morning and between spasms I was able to get the latest news from Alberta.

−*Wainwright Star,* December 27, 1916

Norman Cook served in Europe until the Armistice on November 11, 1918. Instead of returning to the newspaper business, he took up farming in the Olds and Sundre area. In 1940, he was elected as a Social Credit MLA, serving three terms in the Alberta Legislature before his death on August 5, 1950.

CHAPTER SEVEN

Influenza and the Post-war Period

W HEN THE SOLDIERS RETURNED TO ALBERTA following their time on the fields of Europe, they found a changed country and province. Mostly because of these men's efforts and sacrifices on the Western front, Canada was now considered a country of its own—not just a Dominion in the British Empire but a nation that could raise and equip its own army. And these Canadians could hold their own. They could fight with the best of them and be integral in the success of a battle, inspiring their allies and putting the fear of God into their enemies.

> *"We armed every man who was capable of bearing arms, cooks, batmen, engineers—everyman was armed—and we made up our minds what we would do. We were determined to hold that line till we died. We would have died where we stood, but in dying we should have killed so many Germans that we would have ended the war."*

> *In those words to Hon. Dr. Cody, minister of education for Ontario while on a visit to the Canadian corps; Gen. Sir Arthur Currie expressed the corps' invincible determination to hold on to Vimy Ridge, the great strategic center of the western front which the Canadians held in the early days of*

the German offensive last spring. Dr. Cody told the Canadian club at a luncheon how the Germans swung past Vimy beyond Cambrai on the south and up the Lys valley on the north, but the Canadians on Vimy held firm, and the rush was stayed.

On another occasion, Gen. Currie said:

"I wouldn't venture to say that the Canadians have done what nobody else could have done but I do venture to say that if we had not done the particular thing that we did do, it would not have been possible to advance. The Canadian corps have been faced with some of the hardest propositions with which any body of fighting men on the west front have been faced with, and they have faced and won."

—*Red Deer Advocate,* November 11, 1918

Although it would take almost two years for the majority of soldiers to be demobilized and sent back home to Alberta, those who did arrive soon after the war's end found a land gripped with fear. The Spanish flu epidemic, which had struck various parts of the world in 1918–19, swept through Alberta in the late summer and fall of 1918 and the early winter of 1919. Like the war, no community was spared the ravages of the flu epidemic. The war had and would have deeper political and economic implications, but the impact of the flu was more personal. While World War I claimed 20 million lives, an estimated 20 to 100 million were killed by the flu epidemic of 1918–19.

In Alberta, one in 15 people were infected (in communities like Drumheller, Pincher Creek, Taber and Legal, it was one in four), and more than 3000 people died from the Spanish flu. That number was more than half the number of Albertans killed in the war, but the war lasted more than four years and the flu primarily struck within a five- to six-week period in the months of October, November and December.

In common with almost every other town in the west, in fact almost the whole of United States and Canada, Youngstown has been visited by Spanish influenza, and has laid siege to a large number of homes.

This is, however, no occasion for alarm over the arrival of the disease here, for it is merely an acute stage of "la grippe," and in the West has not proved dangerous as in the damp climate of the East, where pneumonia is apt to follow if care is not taken on recovery of the patient.

It is wise however, for people to take every care, both those who are suffering from the disease and those who may take it. Those who know they have it should be careful not to go out into the cold and run risk of a relapse, while people whom it has not yet affected should endeavor to stave off the disease by keeping themselves in good bodily condition.

On Wednesday morning the public school was closed, as a number of the pupils were laid up and it was deemed in the best interest of the public health to adopt this measure.

–Youngstown Plaindealer, October 17, 1918

Messrs. T. E. McIntyre and A.L. Insley are suffering from a mild attack of influenza. These two cases are very mild but on their discovery were immediately isolated by Dr. Mac-Charles. On discovery of the first case on Saturday, the theatre, pool halls, barber shops and schools were closed.

No further cases appearing, it was decided to take the restriction off the business places on Wednesday. Cards have been placed in conspicuous places requested the public not to spit on sidewalks, also when coughing to make use of their handkerchiefs. By the rigid observance of the public of this caution it is expected that the disease may be prevented from spreading and that the town may be made safe for the farmer and his family to come in and do their trading. The public will easily see the necessity for these precautions. It is much better to live up to a few restrictions than the way should be left open for sickness to become prevalent. On it rests the safety of the community.

–*Empress Express*, October 24, 1918

In response to the flu epidemic, schools and churches were closed, and public gatherings, even celebrations for the end of the war, were postponed, and businesses closed or limited their hours of operations. Some towns declared that all residents wear a mask when outside their homes, and in some cases, whole towns were quarantined or required that any persons stepping off the train had to remain in town until such time as the epidemic abated.

The difference between the war and the flu epidemic was that, with the Spanish flu, no one was exempt. In the war, the casualties were men, most under the age of 35, or those innocent and unfortunate civilians who were caught, through no fault of their own, in the crossfire of nations battling for control of Europe. This didn't minimize the tragedy of the war or the sorrow people felt when a loved one or a neighbour was killed in Europe, but the Spanish influenza epidemic literally hit everybody. It struck anywhere and anyone—male and female, young and old, farmer and townsperson—and usually without warning.

In some families, every member was affected, and one or two died, but there could also be one person who suffered no ill effects at all. In other families, only one member became sick while the others remained healthy. And when the flu did strike, it usually hit quickly. For many, death came quickly. In the morning they had the symptoms of a mild cold, and by nightfall they had a fever and were bedridden. Within a day or two, they died. Previous epidemics had taken the very young or the elderly, but with the Spanish flu, people in the prime of their lives and in

Three unidentified Alberta men wearing masks during the Spanish flu epidemic

good health often died. No one was safe; the Spanish flu, as it came to be called, was indiscriminate in its choice of victims.

> *Mrs. Smith, who went to Kingman this afternoon, telephoned just as we were going to press that a nephew, Mr. Tellefaon, died at 3 o'clock. She also reports that they have taken the Lutheran Church and converted into a temporary hospital. The other cases in the Thompson household have already been moved into the church and are in the care of a nurse. The church will be available for any other cases in the district needing hospital attention.*
>
> *Last night a message came that Eric Broen, the youngest son of John Broen of Hay Lakes had died and that all the rest of*

the family, including three brothers, one sister and the mother are very ill.

A few days ago a Mrs. Anderson in the Lake Demay district died from the disease and doctors this morning reported not less than six or eight cases in the district that are practically hopeless.

In face of the inroads which the epidemic is making, all people are once more urged to observe the rules and regulations of the health board, to voluntarily establish absolute quarantines where ever the disease outbreaks and to eliminate all visiting and as far as possible keep the district isolated...

–*Camrose Canadian*, November 7, 1918

Words cannot express the shock and sorrow with which this whole community received the news that Miss Margaret Ada (Maggie) Woods, known and loved by all in town and district, had passed away on Sunday morning, a victim of an attack of the prevailing epidemic. It was reported that Maggie's condition was serious, but none realized that the end was so near, and hopes were entertained for her recovery, but it was otherwise ordained, however, and the Great Reaper again triumphed over all that science and loving care could do to avert the passing away of the loved one; and on Sunday morning this kind and generous-hearted young girl breathed her last.

Miss Woods was born in Sheffield twenty-five years and three months ago, coming to this country with her parents early in the colony's history. She leaves to mourn her loss, besides a sorrowing community, her parents Mr. And Mrs. G.C. Woods, two sisters, Mrs. Harold Huxley and Mrs. Arthur Howell, and two brothers.

The funeral was held on Tuesday, interment being made in the Lloydminster Cemetery.

The Times *in publishing this brief obituary notice, feels a distinct sense of personal loss in the demise of this bright young life, so full of promise, and extends condolences to the sorrowing family.*

–Lloydminster Times, November 21, 1918

Despite the death and sorrow, some people still tried to keep their heads up, still tried to find the good, or at least something to laugh about, during a difficult time.

There isn't much to be said in favour of the masks, which we all have been dutifully wearing for some weeks past. The Observer *doubts very much if they have the slightest efficacy in warding off the influenza, except possibly when one is in a sick-room with a patient. Still, behold, it is an order so let us keep obeying it. It costs only a few cents and a few intense abjurations when a fellow starts out from home without a mask and has to walk back a block or so to get it.*

Yet there is still something to be said in favour of the masks. We have noticed with deep satisfaction that certain of our acquaintances are really looking better with the mask on and the only suggestion we could make would be that they increase the size of the mask and still further beautify their appearance.

–Vegreville Observer, November 20, 1918

In the same issue, the paper continued its editorial comment on the epidemic, praising the women who put themselves at risk by caring for those who had contracted the deadly virus.

The Observer *cannot help being lavish in praise in the unselfish and thorough way in which the ladies of this town have distinguished themselves in caring for the sick during the past three or four weeks. We do not dare mention names lest inadvertently some should be left out and it would take us weeks to get square with them. Nevertheless it is not out of place to call special attention to the public school teachers who with one accord volunteered their service and have rendered indefatigable and invaluable assistance during the epidemic. The same thing holds true of the nuns at the separate school and convent; their zeal in service has be unexcelled. Nor can the assistance be overlooked of those who found it impossible to leave their homes. They, too, helped with all their power in providing necessaries for the sick.*

The record of mutual helpfulness is a striking tribute to the feeling of humanity which actuates all of us. The Observer *is sure that in expressing gratitude to these noble hearted women, it is but voicing the general sentiment of the community.*

God bless them and keep them safe from all the perils which they have voluntarily assumed in the service of others.

–Vegreville Observer, November 20, 1918

As noted in this and other editorials, women—as teachers, nurses, mothers, wives and daughters—played a major role in the care of others suffering during the epidemic. By the time the flu struck Alberta and before the end of World War I, the role of women was changing in the province.

When many of Alberta's men went to fight the war in Europe in 1914, women in the province did not have the right to vote. But by the time the Armistice was signed in 1918 that had changed.

In April 1916, only a few weeks behind Manitoba and Saskatchewan, the Alberta legislature, headed by Premier Arthur Lewis Sifton, granted women the right to vote. Originally, Sifton wasn't keen on the idea, saying that while rural women were interested in voting, elections would cost twice as much to run if women were allowed to vote. But following a major rally in Edmonton, and suffrage legislation being passed in

Arthur L. Sifton, premier of Alberta from 1910 to 1917

Manitoba and Saskatchewan, Sifton gave into the inevitable and backed the legislation.

> *The Sifton government has many good and important Acts passed for the benefit of this province. Democracy has been the watchword of the present government as a synopsis of some of the acts passed will show.*
>
> *The act providing for woman suffrage reads as follow: "Notwithstanding any provisions there in contained, woman shall be on an absolute equality with and have the same rights and privileges and be subject to the same penalties and disabilities as men."*
>
> *–Grande Prairie Frontier*, May 18, 1916

Most newspapers had little or nothing to say for or against the idea of women voting. A good number ran the Act verbatim along with many other Acts passed during the sitting of the Legislature. But the true impact of the new legislation occurred a year later when Alberta became the first province, dominion or territory in the British Empire to elect a woman to a legislative body.

Louise Crummy was born in 1868 in Frankville, Ontario, the sixth child in a family of 10. For a number of years she was a teacher, moving from Ontario to join a sister in North Dakota. While she taught in the U.S., she became deeply involved in the temperance movement, organizing for the Woman's Christian Temperance Union (WCTU). During this time, she met James McKinney. They married, had a son, and in 1903 moved to Claresholm, Alberta. The couple became key members in the community, founding that area's first Methodist Church and a local chapter of the WCTU. McKinney worked with this group for over 20 years, becoming the president of the Canadian chapter and vice-president of the international chapter.

Although Louise McKinney played a major role in the development of a Temperance Act passed by the Sifton government, she also supported the suffrage act. And once women received the right to vote, she decided to run for the Claresholm seat in the legislature as a representative for the newly established Non-Partisan League (NPL). The NPL was formed because it was thought that the traditional parties, the Liberals and Conservatives, did not truly represent farmers and the rural vote. The NPL later became the United Farmers of Alberta (UFA).

McKinney's entry into the election was not exactly welcomed by the local paper, which made no bones about supporting Premier Arthur Sifton and his ruling Liberals.

> *The attitude of some of the ladies during the political campaign has been rather disappointing. Practically all of them lined up with one or other of the political parties. This, of course, is*

what we expected, and as it should be. Many of them have been quite busy in speaking on the platform against the election of certain male candidates. In fact, a lady speaker could be found to speak against any male candidate in the country. When, however, it came to speaking against one of their own sex, they all fell down, and not one woman could be found in the whole province who would appear on the platform against the one woman in the province who sought a position in the legislature. If a woman, because she is a woman, is to have opposition from their sex, whatever party they represented, it amounts to a combine amongst the woman, which in the end, would give the legislature over to them entirely. If the women persist in this attitude, the men of necessity will have to form a combine as well.

–*Claresholm Review-Advertiser,* June 8, 1917

But when McKinney defeated the Liberal candidate (and the others as well) in Claresholm by a decisive margin, the *Review-Advertiser* became more magnanimous. Especially when the event became known and celebrated around the world.

Now that the election is safe and we know the Government is safe, we are not sorry that Mrs. McKinney was elected. We will go even further than that and say we are glad. Mrs. McKinney is bigger than her party. Her party will gain strength because of her, whilst she won't gain anything because of her party. The legislature will be better for her presence and she will exercise a helpful influence in the house. Mrs. McKinney is a woman of mature thought, wide and ripe experience. She has an objective point in view and will steer by that compass. She is a splendid example of consecrated womanhood, not only Claresholm, but all Alberta, is proud of her, and have considerable confidence in her judgment.

Louise McKinney played a major role in the development of a Temperance Act passed by the Sifton government, and she also supported the suffrage act.

Mrs. McKinney's election to the Alberta legislature has put Claresholm on the political map of Canada. News of this even has been spread broadcast over the civilized world. It is some honour to be the first woman to be elected to sit in a British Legislative Assembly which ought to afford some consolation to our defeated liberal candidate. Claresholm has gained some glory by his eclipse behind a skirt.

–Claresholm Review-Advertiser, June 15, 1917

McKinney's election was the beginning of the end of the Alberta Liberal Party that had ruled the land since 1905, the year Alberta became a province. Although McKinney was defeated by independent Thomas Milner in Claresholm in a later election in 1921, the UFA unexpectedly defeated the Liberals in that same election, becoming only the second party to rule in Alberta since provincehood was granted. Even though the UFA didn't run candidates in any of the major cities, it still managed to win 38 of the 58 seats up for grabs. The Liberals came second with 15 seats and would never regain power in the 20th century.

> *The farmer movement has taken on a surprising amount of strength throughout the province. Premier Steward [sic] is the only cabinet minister to an acclamation while about forty United Farmers are in the field.*
>
> *Whatever the result, it is certain that the farmers will have a big say in the next legislature, if not in power. All of the constituencies are being keenly contested, and many reports go to show the farmers will return their candidates by large majorities.*
>
> *–Ponoka Herald,* July 1921

Although the *Herald's* support of the UFA helped the local candidate Reverend Percival Baker to get elected, it was only for a short time. A few weeks before the election, Baker was injured when a tree fell on him. He was bedridden for a time, and on the date of the election his condition seemed to be improving. He died, however, a couple of days after he was elected.

One of key members of the Liberal government, Duncan Marshall, was also the owner of the *Olds Gazette.* Marshall was born in Elderslie Township, Ontario, in 1872. He was a teacher and, later, a publisher/editor of newspapers. He came to Alberta to manage the *Edmonton Bulletin,* but settled in Olds after buying the *Gazette* and establishing the Gazette Publishing Company in 1909. That same year, he was elected as the first MLA of Olds District and was appointed by Alexander Cameron Rutherford as the Provincial Secretary and the Minister of Agriculture. He remained in those positions until 1921. While in government, Marshall operated the *Olds Gazette* through a resident manager.

Duncan Marshall, formerly of the *Edmonton Bulletin* and *Olds Gazette*, 1911

Several Alberta newspapers such as the *Gazette* were supporters of either the Liberal or Conservative party, and many of them were caught off-guard and annoyed by the election of the UFA, even though the people who elected the UFA to power were primarily farmers.

> *The saddest lesson that the new government will have to learn will be the number of things that they can't do and that can't be done by legislation.*

> –*Nanton News*, July 21, 1912

But Marshall, although probably disappointed, held no grudges, according to an *Edmonton Bulletin* story reprinted on the front page of the *Gazette* soon after the election.

Interior view of printing office of the *Olds Gazette*, undated

Hon. Duncan Marshall is not at all disposed to be crushed by his defeat at the polls in the Monday election, and when seen at his office Tuesday morning, said he had nothing to regret. He did not believe that the people had anything against him personally nor against the Stewart government, it was merely a matter of being caught in the wave of conditions that accentuated class consciousness among the U.F.A. party.

Mr. Marshall believed his department, and, in fact, all the departments of the government are in the best possible condition, and it will just remain for the new minister to shape the policies.

Mr. Marshall will continue his farming and livestock activities at Olds, and states he will be very busy the remainder of

the year, as he has numerous invitations to speak and also to judge livestock in the United States.

"I have held this position for fourteen years," said the minister, "and that is longer, with one exception, than any minister of agriculture has been in office in the Dominion. I believe I can say, without boasting, that we have done some good work in this department. If the people want a change, that is their privilege."

–Olds Gazette, July 22, 1921

Marshall sold his interests in the *Olds Gazette* in 1923 to a group headed by Frank Bower, one of the paper's resident managers. Marshall returned to politics in 1934 as a member of the Ontario Legislature and that province's Minister of Agriculture. In 1938, he was named to the Canadian Senate, a post he held until his death in 1946.

Frank Bower and his partners ran the *Olds Gazette* until 1936, when it was sold to William Miller. The Miller family, through William's son-in-law Neil Leatherdale, and Neil's children, ran the *Olds Gazette* until the paper and its printing operation was sold to Mountain View Publishing in 2005. Immediately following the sale, the *Gazette* was amalgamated with the *Mountain View County News* to become the *Mountain View Gazette.*

But following the political and influenza battles, Alberta in the early 1920s seemed to be on the verge of great prosperity. And for many years, it did grow and expand. With their own party in power, the rural areas of the province felt more in control of their destinies. As a result, the agriculture industry expanded and diversified, especially into the dairy and livestock industries. Turner Valley was on the verge of another oil boom, and Alberta's coal industry, despite some union difficulties, grew to become the largest supplier of coal in the country. Weekly newspapers also came into their own during this time.

Left to right: A.L. Horton, Neil Leatherdale and Sam Hodgson, Lethbridge, 1946

~

After the economic downturn of the second decade of the century, the horrors of the Great War and the grief of the Spanish flu epidemic, good times had finally arrived in Alberta.

It was, unfortunately, short-lived. Hard times were only a few years away.

~

Claresholm newspapers began in 1904, and as the settlement continued to grow, the *Claresholm Review* was established, with Woodburn McDonald as the editor.

The first issue of the *Claresholm Advertiser* was published on Wednesday, April 15, 1914. The *Review-Advertiser* came into publishing on January 13, 1919, with F.H Schooley as editor; the last issue was printed on May 4, 1928.

The *Claresholm Local Press*, Volume 1, No. 1, was printed on October 8, 1926, with Rae King, known as R.L. King, as editor and publisher.

The building was located on what is now 49th Avenue W. In 1928, King bought a lot on Second Street, the present location of the paper. A cottage roof building, 24 feet by 24 feet, was constructed and became the publishing house of the *Claresholm Local Press*. The last copy showing R.L. King as editor was dated December 21, 1944.

Gordon Neale bought the *Claresholm Local Press* from King and printed the first issue on January 4, 1945. In 1946 he bought the mailing list of the *Stavely Advertiser* with 350 subscribers. Both papers were then printed in Claresholm.

In 1948, more room was needed for additional equipment so an extra 24 feet was added to the back of the building. In 1954 a 10-foot-by-48-foot addition was built onto the north side of the building to store paper stock and to make room for an automatic folder for the paper. A 14- by 18-foot office was later built on the south side of the original building.

Eldon ("Andy") G. Anderson bought the paper from Gordon Neale and took possession on February 1, 1965. At the time of the purchase, the paper was still being printed by letterpress, meaning all the type had to be set by hand, Linotype or engraved in lead before it went to the press to be printed. All setting of type and press runs were done in Claresholm except for press ion colour printing. Both the *Claresholm Local Press* and the *Stavely Advertiser* were printed this way.

After the last issue of the *Stavely Advertiser* was printed, the *Stavely News* was included in the Claresholm paper. The last paper to be printed in the original building was on July 27, 1972, at which time the present building was built in two stages. The back half was built first. The printing equipment was moved into its new quarters, and while the front half was being built, the office was run from the Dr. Morley Hodgson building across the street next to the post office.

The official opening of Cedar Terrace, which now houses the *Claresholm Local Press*, the Video Place and four suites upstairs, was held on March 24, 1973.

June 5, 1975, marked a change of history for the *Claresholm Local Press*. The electronic age took over the mechanical working equipment. A computer called "Linocomp," with a regular typewriter keyboard of 36-plus keys, was installed that replaced the mechanical

Linotype keyboard of 90 keys. The Linocomp was a photoelectric computer; the second of its kind in Alberta that set type on photograph paper. The pages were paper paste-ups; negatives were developed in a newly built dark room and sent out for printing on an offset press. Updated computers were changed approximately every two years to keep up with new developments in printing.

On April 1, 1978, Paul W. Rockley bought the *Claresholm Local Press* from E.G. Anderson. In 1989, three SE30 computers and a laser writer printer were purchased, moving the paper into the computer age.

Rockley also bought the *Okotoks Western Wheel* in June 1989 and was editor and publisher of both papers, dividing his time between Claresholm and Okotoks until selling the *Claresholm Local Press* in 1990. Rockley was involved in organizing the Claresholm Christmas Hamper Program, which still helps many celebrate a happier Christmas to this day.

EMS Press Ltd. purchased the *Claresholm Local Press* on March 30, 1990, with George

Meyer and Gordon Scott becoming partners. Scott took the helm of publisher and editor until April 2000. In 1998, a retirement party was held to honour Roy Pachal's long-time employment of 45 years at the paper, the longest tenure in the newspaper's history.

During Scott's tenure as editor, the *Claresholm Local Press* was changed to tabloid size in 1995 and pagination was done completely by computer. Scott also brought in full-colour printing to Claresholm by purchasing a laser digital colour printer called a Docu Press. Gordon Scott passed away suddenly in his home on April 4, 2000.

The year 2000 also saw another change at the paper. Negatives no longer had to be shot, and the paper was sent to press electronically.

From April 2000 to June 2005, George Meyer became sole owner of the *Claresholm Local Press*.

Gradually, the *Local Press* moved into the digital age, closing its darkroom for good in 2004 with the purchase of two excellent digital cameras.

On July 1, 2005, the latest chapter in the *Local Press'* long history began when Roxanne Thompson purchased the paper after being with the organization for 20 years.

The year 2005 also marked the 100th anniversary of the Town of Claresholm and the Province of Alberta. The *Local Press* celebrated the occasion by publishing a special 44-page commemorative edition.

CHAPTER EIGHT

The Great Depression

HISTORICALLY, THE GREAT DEPRESSION began on Black Tuesday, October 29, 1929, when the New York Stock Exchange collapsed. While major corporations suffered much because of the market crash, the effects of the Depression took some time to trickle down to Alberta and its smaller communities. Even so, Albertans were already suffering some doldrums before 1928, and there were worries that the low times would continue. Some predicted even further hardships ahead but also understood that Alberta's strength of character would see the province through what became some of the toughest economic years in its history.

> *The year 1928, with its bright hopes and somber disappointment; its high aims, worthy endeavors, and scant achievements, has run its course; it has tottered over the borderline which tells off the fleeting years, and one more milestone along that journey which can never be retraced, has left behind forever.*
>
> *Most of our farmers and many of our business men have had to wage their battle against tremendous odds during the past season; their reserves have had to be called in, and difficulties have been encountered in even holding their own. Men of the north, however, are not permanently overthrown by reason*

*of one or two, or even a number of reserves; the year 1929
will witness another and even a more strenuous endeavor and
oftentimes, victory is wrested out of the very jaws of defeat.*

–*Lloydminster Times*, January 3, 1929

Hard times did come to Alberta, though, and the so-called men of
the North had their reserves tested over and over again. First wheat prices
plummeted while prices for farming supplies and equipment remained the
same. Farmers who had borrowed based on higher gains defaulted on their
loans. Many farms that had survived for generations went under, and soon,
so did several of the businesses in the small towns that supported them.

The worldwide demand for coal also dropped significantly, and the
mines throughout the provinces, especially those in the Crowsnest Pass
area and near Hinton, had to shut down, putting many people out of work.
And when the effects of the stock market crash finally reached Alberta,
many banks, most with head offices in the eastern part of Canada, refused
to offer loans, foreclosed on others. Hundreds of businesses, small and
large, went bankrupt. Everywhere, people, men mostly, were thrown out
of work, the prospects for their future extremely dim. Many were unem-
ployed for months or even years at a time, and families were uprooted
from homes and farms that had supported them for generations. Lives
were torn apart and people suffered.

*There is an S.O.S cry of distress going up from all over the
West, and unless something is done—and done quickly—there
will be actual starvation going on this winter in many a home.
Trade and commerce are almost at a standstill; as A cannot
pay B because C has not paid him; and at the present time
the West has to finance without the assistance of the banks.
The number of cases of actual hardship that have come to our
personal notice is terrible. The thresher cannot pay his men
because the farmer has not paid him, being unable to dispose
of his grain and several of these men have been walking our*

Echo newspaper building on the right, Athabasca, 1966

streets absolutely without a cent in their pockets and without food, with no place to sleep to make matters worse.

–Lloydminster Times, November 27, 1930

On top of the financial catastrophes, there were also natural disasters, some of almost biblical proportions. The wheat-growing belts of Central and Southern Alberta that many early explorers had called a possible "bread basket to the world" suffered from terrible drought. Months, and in some cases years, passed with only a few inches of rain. This created conditions ripe for dust storms and wildfires. Other areas of the province received too much rain, causing serious flooding. And if flooding wasn't a problem and crops grew, then clouds of grasshoppers in clusters so thick they blocked out the sun, swooped down and ate all vegetation in sight.

Winter also saw blizzards and cold snaps so deep and strong that even survivors from the years of early settlement were surprised by their severity. A 1935 edition of the *Athabasca Echo* reported more than

85 days of sub-zero weather, including several days when thermometers that could measure past 60° below had simply frozen. It seemed that Mother Nature was unleashing her wrath on the North American landscape, especially in the prairies.

> *Friday's sun fell on a rather desolate-looking village, as the waters of the big Wayne flood receded, and the occupants of more than a hundred homes, which were under water, began the gigantic task of re-establishing themselves. The men were busy trying to get their house back on the right lots and recovering their chicken houses, and the other buildings. Houses were filled with mud as water receded, furniture and bedding were ruined, and gardens washed out. Many of the hundred houses were warped, some shifted from their foundations for over forty feet. Three houses on one lot were turned end over end, while smaller places drifted entirely away. One pigeon house went down the Rosebud in a straight up position and when it hit the first bridge, it smashed to pieces and the frightened pigeons all flew away.*

> *The first bridge out of Rosedale was washed out and is end down in Rosebud Creek. All the others between Rosedale and Wayne, on the splendid highway, have the approaches more or less washed out.*

> *The water situation at Wayne is causing alarm, as the wells have all been contaminated, many caving in and being filled with muck and filth. Sergeant Skelton, of the Alberta Provincial Police, was in charge of the situation, and every man from the Drumheller detachment spent the greater part of Friday at Wayne attending to the relief of the homeless.*

> *–Drumheller Review, June 25, 1931*

> *The rain was surely welcome but it was too bad the drop in ground temperature played that trick on us when the first*

Alberta publishers at a newspaper conference in Calgary in the early 1940s

showers came. It froze as it came down and not for many years has a similar sight been witnessed. Everything was coated with an inch of clean ice, the weight being tremendous.

A few trees in town suffered minor damages locally to light and power lines but the telephone system was laid out, almost every single pole in town and district going down.

They lay sprawling in every direction amidst a tangled mass of wire. When one compares the slender thin pole used, and the tremendous weight they were carrying, one wonders how they stood up at all. They have evidently long been a serious menace and danger and we did not know it.

–Three Hills Capital, April 28, 1932

The fierce dust storm which raged all day Monday put a stop to the holding of the sports which were advertised to be held here. After deliberating for some time, the baseball teams from Delia and Craigmyle played a game which was the only sport attraction of the day and quite a large crowd braved the elements, mostly in the shelter of cars to watch it.

–*Hanna Herald*, May 28, 1931

All of these elements only exacerbated the difficulties of the Great Depression. While many Albertans struggled through, a good number of others reached their breaking point.

The life of Frank Amatto for a great many years resident of Blairmore, came to a tragic ending yesterday afternoon when he made use of a single barrel shotgun to blow his brains out.

His family were in an adjoining room when the rash act was perpetrated. Police and doctors were immediately summoned and found the prostrate body laying in a pool of blood, while the top of his head was scattered to all parts of the room.

Worry over lack of employment was given as a cause.

–*Blairmore Enterprise*, January 5, 1933

Newspapers in Alberta suffered as well. Bad times for farmers and small town businesses resulted in a dearth of advertising and a drop in print jobs. But the prices for all the essentials for a successful publication—paper, ink, wages, postage—remained at the same levels, creating a difficult situation throughout the industry. Between 1929 and 1937, more than 50 weekly newspapers folded, including some that had been operating since the early years of the province.

In order to show the plight of the weekly newspaper, *Drumheller Review* editor Archie Key half-jokingly called for a moratorium on newspaper publishing. "Let every newspaper close down until business picks up—if it can," he wrote. "Allow every gossip on the townsite the freedom of the streets and telephone; make it necessary for every politician to glorify himself single-handed; let the public do its own guessing as to what is happening throughout the civilized world."

Key left the *Review* in 1936 and the paper just barely made it out of the Depression, finally folding in 1940.

One paper, however, suffered a huge loss during the Depression but managed to literally pull itself out of the fire. Herbert George McCrea was born in Peterborough, Ontario, in 1892. In 1910 he moved to Saskatchewan but came to Alberta in 1911 as part of a mining survey gang in the Rocky Mountains. For a short time he worked for the *Langdon Leader*, but in 1912 he purchased the Washington hand press of that paper from Leonard Nesbitt and founded the *Hanna Herald*, its first edition appearing on Christmas Eve of that year.

For more than two decades, the *Herald* was the premier paper of this central Alberta town, and McCrea became known for the high quality of his editorials. From 1927 to 1937, McCrea also held the office of Secretary of the Alberta division of the Canadian Weekly Newspapers Association (CWNA), one of longest serving secretaries in the association's history.

Hanna suffered greatly during the Depression, enduring a long drought, with dust storms, wildfires and grasshoppers. But the *Herald* continued to publish an issue every Thursday, with McCrea's editorials supporting ideas of relief and help for the family farm and the working man. Around midnight on February 20, 1935, three days after the paper's weekly issue was published, a fire started on a stove in the onetime home of the local Elks Lodge, located on the second floor of the *Herald* building. The fire burned for almost an hour before a mechanic noticed it.

By the time the local volunteer fire department arrived, flames were blowing through the second floor windows and bursting through the roof. Despite the efforts of firefighters, the second floor collapsed, completely destroying the offices and printing plant of the *Hanna Herald*. Damage was estimated at $18,000.

Even with this major setback, McCrea and the staff of the *Herald* soldiered on. They missed printing a few issues, but within a month of the fire, the paper returned with a six-page issue featuring a front-page editorial of appreciation and determination.

> *After labouring in this field for almost 20 years, developing a newspaper of which we are proud and forming a business connection which we value highly, the loss caused by fire has naturally proved a real shock. But, in spite of this loss and the inconvenience resulting, we can see only one logical course to follow. That is to CARRY ON.*
>
> *Immediately after the fire, we decided to rebuild and get re-established as quickly as possible. We have exerted every effort to this end and in the face of tremendous difficulties, we believe that the resumption of publication within four weeks is an achievement which reflects no little credit upon the workmen who have rallied around us.*
>
> *To our brother newspapermen of the province, we say that their sincere interest in our welfare was something which prompted us to move quickly, square our shoulders and prepare to rebuild. To those who have assisted the* Herald *in handling its printing orders, we extend profound thanks. The* Drumheller Mail *and the* Banff Crag and Canyon *especially, have been of invaluable assistance to us in this connection.*
>
> *Finally, we can only say that we still have unbounded faith in our people. We believe that our country will see the return of prosperity. WE INTEND TO CARRY ON.*
>
> –*Hanna Herald*, March 24, 1935

Herbert McCrea remained as editor of the *Herald* until his death in 1937. His wife Hazel and son Bob took over the publication. Hazel also took over Herbert's duties as secretary of the CWNA, remaining in the position until 1942. The *Hanna Herald* remained in the McCrea family until the death of Bob McCrea in 1981. It later became part of the Bowes newspaper chain.

As stated earlier, Herbert McCrea was noted for the quality of his editorials. By the time the following editorial was written, the last before his death, the Great Depression was beginning to wane. Times, though, were still hard. McCrea's editorial was reprinted in many papers throughout the province and truly captured the hardships and the strength of the human spirit that allowed Alberta to weather one of its greatest storms during those years.

It is not an easy matter for the editor, living in the midst of a farming area which has suffered severely from drought for several years, to speak words of hope and comfort to our people. We are too near the picture to take an abstract viewpoint.

"The toad beneath the harrow knows

Exactly where each tooth point goes

The butterfly upon the road

Preached contentment to the toad"

In this instance we are all under the harrow of drouth and we feel its sharp points. Every citizen in the area whether drouth had wrought ruination is in that position.

At the same time we feel despair should not go unchallenged. Nothing can be accomplished by adding to the blackness of the situation. Our people have shown a Spartan endurance that is almost unbeatable. They have not all curled up.

The people have learned to tighten their belts and take a licking standing up. There is less calamity howling around here than in the Ontario newspapers who are consigning the west to the waste basket.

Two inches of rain the last of June would have changed the picture around here completely. We all know that. Our country can produce a crop with very little rain. And it's going to rain in seasons to come.

Help and encouragement will be needed. There is nothing to be gained by making things bluer than they really are. Let's all do what we can to lighten each other's burdens. That will make the load a little easier for all.

Let's not all get panicky. Outsiders, it seems, are more prone to such a line of action than the people living right here. Let calmer counsel and wiser action prevail. Let us take for our motto the admonition of a commander of a famous British regiment,

Steady the Buffs.

–Hanna Herald, June 1937

The history of newspapers in Stony Plain and area, leading to the establishment of the *Stony Plain Reporter*, is somewhat uncertain. Many of the dates in *Alberta Newspapers 1880–1982: An Historical Directory* by Gloria Strathern, for example, are followed by question marks.

Based on her information, however, it appears the *Stony Plain Advertiser and Lac Ste. Anne Reporter* began publishing on December 9, 1909. The paper carried on for years under that name before becoming simply the *Stony Plain Advertiser*.

The *Advertiser* appears to have ceased operation for approximately six months, before starting up again half a year later and surviving for about two years.

The *Stony Plain News*, started a few months after the *Advertiser's* demise and seemingly lasting less than a year, stopped publication on October 23, 1914.

The *Mirror* tried to make a go of it on May 6, 1915, but it also lasted only about one year.

For three years the community seems to have been without a paper, until the *Stony Plain Herald* began publishing in 1919, but again only for a year.

The *Stony Plain Sun* came along in 1920 and published for about 18 years before the *Stony Plain Reporter* started up on April 6, 1945. And by this time, the historical records no longer appear tentative and uncertain.

Stony Plain Advertiser editor and publisher William Worton put news of council meetings, concerts, dances, church suppers and agricultural meetings on the front page. Other pages were devoted to world news and news from the communities of Blueberry, Manly, Wabamun, Mewassin, Brightbank, Keephills, Glory Hills, Pine Ridge, Golden Spike and Spruce Grove.

A column carried for several issues visualized Stony Plain in 1930 as a community with a brick hotel that had revolving doors, a radial railway carrying passengers from the station to the city park and an imposing building with the sign "Stony Plain Agricultural Society" over the door.

Advertisements touted men's patent leather shoes for $4.50 and overalls for $1.

The first editor of the *Stony Plain Reporter* was W.H. "Duke" DeCoursey, who was also owner and general manager of the operation.

In his book, *The Yellowknife Years*, DeCoursey talks about the difficulty of running newspapers in those days.

"Wartime conditions had imposed restrictions on the manufacturing of printing machinery. We (Maude and I) learned in Toronto that only one rebuilt linotype was on the Canadian market for sale list. It was in Winnipeg, and we bought it without seeing it, for Yellowknife."

Almost as an afterthought, he adds, "We bought also the printing plant and building in Stony Plain, Alberta, that had housed a weekly operation by then out of business for several years."

Some pages later, he remarks, "I had convinced myself that I had thrown $900 down the drain when I bought the lot, building and newspaper equipment at Stony Plain.

"I decided that I should resell my poor buy if I could."

After actually managing to get a considerably better offer, though, he was "encouraged by business people to establish a weekly newspaper there also."

DeCoursey and his wife ended up living in an apartment above the printing plant. The first edition of DeCoursey's Yellowknife paper, *News of the North*, came off the Stony Plain press in early May 1945.

"We were developing the two new publications at the same time..." and "my father, living in Rimbey, came out of retirement to call on, I believe, every farmer within the Stony Plain area. Within a few months the *Reporter* had a net paid circulation of about 700."

Editor and publisher Walter Mandick purchased the paper on April 30, 1962, and eventually sold it to Lynard Publishers Ltd.

Lynard was purchased by Bowes Publishers Ltd. in the mid-1980s, and Bowes was eventually purchased by Sun Media Corporation, a Quebecor company.

The *Stony Plain Reporter* now has a circulation of almost 10,000 and is published in conjunction with the *Spruce Grove Examiner*, with a circulation of close to 9000.

The *Examiner* was established in 1970 and purchased by Lynard Publishers on June 1, 1982, from Terry and Florence Clements, owners of Grove Publishing Ltd.

CHAPTER NINE

Alberta Weeklies and the
Ku Klux Klan

THE SAME YEAR THE GREAT DEPRESSION is said to have begun, another ugly entity entered the Alberta landscape.

On July 12, 1929, the leader of the Saskatchewan branch of the Ku Klux Klan (the KKK), John James Maloney, marched in a parade in Vermilion. Although Maloney noted that he was only there to support the local Orange Lodge, the appearance of a burning cross in town later that night indicated something different. Although the KKK had made some minor recruitment efforts in southern Alberta in the early 1920s, Maloney's appearance at such a prominent event showed that the KKK was serious about expanding into Alberta.

A few months later, R.C. Snelgrove, a Klan organizer also from Saskatchewan, went on a speaking tour throughout Alberta, claiming that he sold a good number of memberships in Alberta, establishing a few Klan branches, called "Klaverns." According to some reports, Alberta membership in the KKK reached 7000, and in 1932, Premier John E. Brownlee, gave the KKK status under the Alberta Societies Act.

Alberta newspapers, however, did not take kindly to the Klan. Many publications, including the *Drumheller Mail*, the *High River Times*, the

Lacombe Western Globe and the *Vegreville Observer*, openly criticized the Klan and their recruiting efforts in the province.

> *It seems strange that so little seems to be learned from observation. For many years Canadians have been privileged to look upon the activities of the Ku Klux Klan in the United States. They have seen the disquietude and disturbance which the organization worked in society. They have seen the ruthless and ignorant forces usurp themselves the right to enforce law. They have seen periods of terrorism exercised by this secret society. Yet they permitted the KKK entrance into Canada.*
>
> –*Vegreville Observer,* June 22, 1932

> *I'm either a degenerate or a Jesuit according to R.C. Snelgrove, who told a slim audience on Saturday that only Jesuit Romanists, bawdy-house keepers, bootleggers and other low-down creatures were opposed to the Ku Klux Klan. Possibly R.C. (please pardon his initials) overlooked communists because I can name a half dozen who are opposed to the Kluck Kluck Kluck.*
>
> *And R.C. (why doesn't he change his initials) said the Klan was misunderstood; that it had been dragged through the garbage by the R.C. (the church, not the man), and the boys didn't wear nightshirts anymore or pillowslips and I gather from his speech that every time a Klansman was thrown into the hoosegow that it was persecution whereas if an adherent of the Pope got pinched, it was justice.*
>
> *He also talks about pure Protestantism and pure patriotism and if I dare to suggest that his principles espoused by the Klan [do] not coincide with my ideas on the subject, I am classed as a bawdy-house keeper—which suggests to me that this purity campaign has its weak points.*
>
> –*Drumheller Mail,* November 28, 1929

Interior view of the *Lacombe Western Globe* newspaper office, 1927

In response to this article, the KKK burned a cross on the lawn of Archie Key, editor of the *Drumheller Mail.*

In the *Lacombe Western Globe*, editor Charles "Barney" Halpin took the fight to the Klan. Halpin had been the news editor of the *Calgary Albertan*, having arrived in Calgary on the first-ever CPR train. He moved to Lacombe in 1903 to found the *Western Globe* and served as the editor until 1935, when he retired to become a printing instructor in Olds. From 1912 to 1913, he also served as the mayor of Lacombe. In response to a Klan-recruiting speech in town, the *Western Globe*, over two issues, ran one letter and nine articles that criticized the Klan. Throughout the winter and into the spring, Halpin continued to fight against the KKK, even organizing a speech by William J. Clark, a former Assistant Treasurer for the State of Kansas who was farming in

Lacombe. Clark had written a letter to the *Western Globe* describing the hateful actions of the Klan in Kansas.

The battle reached its peak in May 1930 when the KKK tarred and feathered a local blacksmith.

> *These hooded hoodlums hide their faces at night so that the world may not know them (as they must consider their work disgraceful) and during the day they mingle with respectable citizens, masquerading as men, which they are most surely not. Mob justice seems to be the watchword of this organization and mob justice is not justice.*
>
> *The law of this land says that every man, no matter his rank or his crime, shall be allowed a fair trial. The Klan, which has no authority whatsoever, seems to have a law unto itself—anyone who is an offender of "their" law is punished in "their" way. They seem to have a very primitive sense of justice, i.e., a bunch of full-grown, able bodied men attack and overpower one unprotected man, apply a coat of tar and feathers—and call it justice. It is a disgrace on the face of it to call these people British. It would be a disgrace to any country to have these men claim that country's nationality.*
>
> *The lawless element in our community have shown just what sort of men they are, and not a stone should be left unturned to bring the offenders to justice. It was a most cowardly deed, and the action of this mob last week stamp them as dangerous to the peace and welfare of our community*
>
> *–Lacombe Western Globe*, May 30, 1930

Immediately, the KKK penned a response to Halpin, stating: "If your present conduct is persisted in you, you will be severely punished therefor. Your place of business and residence will be burned to the ground. You will be glad to leave Lacombe before the K.K.K. is through with you,

Charles B. Halpin of *Lacombe Western Globe*, 1911

if any further slanderous statements are indulged in." Halpin published the letter verbatim in the paper and added his editorial comment.

> *Threatening letters are one method these Hooded Cowards make use of to intimidate those who dare to oppose them in their nefarious acts, but only a fool will pay any attention to that method of procedure.*
>
> *The K.K.K. has no place in Alberta; the type of men who rally around their fiery cross are not of the calibre any place would want to enforce their laws. Most of them could not get into a decent lodge if they did wish to, and the rest are "blind fools" who have been talked into something their better judgment should have warned them against.*
>
> *—Lacombe Western Globe,* June 6, 1930

Halpin's home and paper remained untouched, and for the next couple of years, he fought against the KKK, giving full coverage to the trial of four men charged with the tarring and feathering, as well as the Edmonton trial against Maloney for break and enter, and insurance fraud. That conviction marked the end of the KKK as a major presence in Alberta.

In an 2003 article, "Upholding Social Decency and Political Equality," Donald Wetherell, an associate professor at the University of Alberta wrote, "For years [Halpin], along with other journalists in the province, had warned about the true character of Maloney and the Alberta Klan. But Halpin's prescience is not what is important about his place in Alberta history. Rather, he showed that respect for human rights and human decency, and the courage to articulate and uphold reason and basic values, could help combat the dark lure of bigotry."

Charles B. (Barney) Halpin passed away in 1951.

≈

The Community Press

Published weekly at 4917 - 50 St. Killam AB.
& 4025 - 47 St. Sedgewick, AB.
**Serving Flagstaff County
and Surrounding areas
for over 103 years**
$1 including GST
Canada

We acknowledge the financial support of the
Government of Canada through the Canada Periodical
Fund (CPF) for our publishing activities.

The Community Press in Sedgewick evolved from the *Sedgewick Sentinel*, which was established in 1908 by A.J. Honey who came to Canada from England.

In 1915, A.L. Eastly purchased the paper and began expanding and buying out other local newspapers. In 1930, he changed the name of the paper to *The Community Press* and began serving all the towns along Highway 13 in the County of Flagstaff.

Arthur "Art" W. Eastly took over the operation of the weekly newspaper from his father in 1942. Art added new equipment and built a new building. With the help of his son Ace, the Eastlys continued running the newspaper until the senior Eastly's retirement.

In 1969, Monte Keith bought the business from Art, ending the 54-year Eastly ownership. The new owner moved the operation from handset type into the modern age of offset in the mid-1970s. In 1975, *The Community Press* encompassed the entire County of Flagstaff, and the purchase of the *Alliance Enterprise* joined the entire Flagstaff area into one news and information district.

In 1977, Rick Truss purchased half of Monte's company, and they installed a web press, an offset camera and new photo equipment. The partnership dissolved in 1985, and Truss took over the entire *Community Press* operation himself.

In 1985, after closing out a partnership with the Keiths in Wainwright, Kerry Anderson came to the paper and entered into partnership with Rick in 1989. One year earlier *The Community Press* moved the newspaper portion of the company to its present Main Street location in Sedgewick.

In 1992, the paper took another technological step forward by purchasing the best desktop publishing programs in the business. The entire system was connected by modem to the Alberta Weekly Newspapers Association office and three mobile units by modem to the main workstation in Sedgewick. Later, of course, the operation used an Internet connection.

In 1993, Truss and Anderson bought out Dick Morris and purchased the *Weekly Review* in Viking.

In 1999, partners Kerry Anderson, Rick Truss, Gary and Maryann Wolosinka and Shelley Rattray bought shares in the *Tofield Mercury*. In 2005, Anderson bought out his partners and became sole proprietor of all the publications, including the *Mercury*. He moved to an acreage in Lindbrook in July 2005 with his wife Michelle and two sons Brennan and Garrett. Anderson appointed Nicole Giasson as editor and manager of the *Tofield Mercury*.

In October 2005, Anderson opened up a newspaper in Lamont called the *Leader*. As well, a 15,000-circulation advertiser called the *East Central Times* that goes out once a month was started.

Over the years, *The Community Press* has won numerous awards for news writing, creative advertising and coverage of the arts. The paper has also been honoured for best Fire Prevention supplement eight times from 1994 to 2004.

The Community Press is most proud of spearheading community fundraising efforts such as organizing supplies for the Manitoba flood victims, collecting supplies for Kosovo refugees and fundraising for tsunami aid and for Hurricane Katrina victims. As well, publisher Kerry Anderson and Michelle Molyneux work as media liaisons for the Canadian Cancer Society with the help of the weekly newspaper industry.

CHAPTER TEN

Bible Bill and the Pulitzer

IN 1935, IN WHAT WOULD HAPPEN only once more in Alberta's past, a new party assumed power in the legislature. Led by charismatic Baptist preacher William "Bible Bill" Aberhart, the Social Credit Party swept the United Farmers of Alberta (UFA) out of the legislature, taking 56 of the 63 seats with 54 percent of the popular vote.

Born on December 20, 1878, in Kippen, Ontario, William Aberhart did not have political ambitions in his early life. His interests lay more in education and religion. He arrived in Calgary to become the principal of Alexandra School in 1910. At the same time, he worked as a lay preacher in the Baptist Church, starting a Sunday bible study course. His charismatic manner attracted more and more people, and by 1925, his message was broadcast throughout the province by the radio station CFCN.

Like many, Aberhart was disheartened by the impact of the Great Depression, especially its effect on farmers in Alberta and Saskatchewan. He was drawn particularly to the Social Credit theories of Major Clifford H. Douglas, which simply stated that government grants should supplement the difference in production costs and an individual's purchasing power, and that institutions such as the banks, the government, the press and others existed to serve the individual and not the other way around.

William Aberhart, premier of Alberta from 1935 to 1943

In the early '30s, Aberhart approached the ruling UFA government to adopt the Social Credit policies in order to help the common people survive the Great Depression. But when his pleas fell on deaf ears, he helped found the Alberta Social Credit Party in 1934, proposing, among other ideas, that every Albertan be given $25 a month to purchase necessities. Unlike many of the other political parties, Aberhart could reach into the homes of most Albertans with his weekly radio broadcast, and he used that platform to promote the ideals of the Social Credit Party.

"Alarmed" is the word that betrays the whole basis of action which blazed forth last Thursday morning in Edmonton press news regarding counter-action Alberta's Social Credit program as outlined by Wm. Aberhart, B.A. of Calgary. I wonder what it is that is giving Mr. Brownlee and other men in

this province so much alarm. And why are they alarmed? Are they afraid that if they cease to function in the "interests" of the people of Alberta that the people are going to suffer. The particular interests, I am able to read, that are interests alarmed, as are the financial interests, and it is quite evident that the other "interests" are also alarmed that finance will be adversely affected if Social Credit is adopted in Alberta. But no one need to be alarmed about their own particular welfare from a social credit regime. We will still be able to produce and consume goods the same way we did before, except that the production and consumption will be speeded up, two, three and four fold when it is made possible for people to get their own products without having to pay exorbitant interest charges for the privilege, as now.

What these gentlemen are "alarmed" about is that the new system will work, and that the old diehards are going to be substituted by a new order which will give the people the results of their own efforts, their own products and put into effect a distribution system intended to be of benefit to the producers and consumers instead of these financial interests who are so terribly "worried."

–*Sedgewick Community Press*, April 18, 1935

The *Sedgewick Community Press* was one of the strongest supporters of Social Credit in the Alberta newspaper industry. Publisher Arthur Le Grande Eastly was originally an American; he was born in the Dakota Territory in 1879 and moved to Wetaskiwin in 1905 to work as a printer for the *Wetaskiwin Times*. In 1915, he bought the *Sedgewick Sentinel* from its founder A.J Honey. For the next 15 years, Eastly expanded his operations, buying out other newspapers in the area: the *Bawlf Sun, Daysland Press, Hardisty Mail, Lougheed Express* and *Strome Despatch*. Eastly, however, was hit hard by the Great Depression, and he sold or lost most of his other papers, except the one in Sedgewick. The Eastly family operated

A.L. Eastly (1911), owner of several Alberta newspapers in the early 1900s

the *Sedgewick Community Press* for over 54 years, until Arthur L. Eastly's son, Arthur Jr., retired and sold the paper in 1969. *The Community Press* is still in operation today.

Eastly and his *Community Press* was such a huge supporter of William Aberhart and Major Douglas' theories about Social Credit that in 1934 and 1935, Eastly ran numerous editorials and articles supporting the party week after week, including a front-page essay written by Aberhart himself. He wrote so much about Social Credit that he once noted, "I have harped on the subject of social credit so much during the past year that I am getting tired of it. I imagine that many of my readers are in the same boat."

A number of Eastly's newspaper contemporaries were not fans of the Social Credit Party and made their views known.

We are sorry to see such an experienced editor put off his balance by an illusory will-'o-the-wisp of political economy. As we have said before, we are all for evolutionary reform, but deplore revolution which never accomplished anything but a general smashing up of the best in men and material. Were Alberta to attempt these senseless inflationary methods it would cut itself adrift from the rest of Canada and the world markets and have to eat our own produce. Like the crazy Nebuchadnezzar we would eat grass like an ox. If Aberhart would only stick to a concrete proposal as to how he would raise the 120 million a year he proposes to give away one could analyze his proposal. First he talks of taxing products and when the producer spouts out that his produce does not realize cost now and how can he pay the new tax, Aberhart springs a new one, he will levy on exports and unearned increments in trade and to hoodwink the farmer promises a just price. Then he would confiscate the savings of the thrifty.

All this indicates and he admits that he has nothing more than an Utopian dream and if you return his candidates they will make him premier and he will employ a gang of experts to evolve something.

It is quite a safe bet that if he had not baited his hook with that $25 he never would have caught so many suckers, and we are sorry to see Editor Eastly so badly hooked.

–Athabasca Echo, June 21, 1935

But support for Social Credit ideals spread, and at the very least, the party represented change, which was what a lot of Albertans were looking for. Farmers, small business owners and other working-class folks were deeply in debt, either bankrupt or close to bankruptcy, and the need for something, anything, to ease their troubles, was urgent.

The ruling UFA also had its own difficulties. In 1934, Premier John E. Brownlee was forced to resign after being found guilty of seducing a young clerk in the Attorney General's office. So following what was called one of the most interesting elections in Alberta history, Social Credit swept to power. More than 80 percent of Alberta's population voted in the election, still the highest voter turnout in the province's history. The former ruling party, the UFA, was completely shut out of the legislature, with the Liberals and Conservatives splitting the remaining seven seats between them. And for the first time ever, people who had been born in Alberta were elected as MLAs.

> *I am not going to crow at the outcome of the election in Alberta. This crowing business is something that was disparaged by our new member, Mr. A.E. Fee, and it has no place now that we are all united, or supposed to be, in our intention of co-operating with the new elected government. Although the first trench has been won, in the election of a Social Credit government in Edmonton, that battle has only started.*
> *—Sedgewick Community Press, August 29, 1935*

While many of Alberta's newspapers were skeptical of Aberhart's Social Credit ideas, they were optimistic about the change his election had brought and were willing to give the new government a chance to apply their theories in the hope that they would work and Alberta would rise from the depths of the Great Depression.

> *It is hoped that the citizens of Alberta will not be disappointed in their choice of government in the recent election. It was a hard fought battle and now that the smoke and grime have cleared away, it is our duty to come forward and offer our congratulations to the victorious social credit forces. The people will have to be patient of course and give the government-elect time to fit themselves into a difficult job. The cooperation of the citizens is needed; their duty has not ended with their vote. They have to stand by and lend every assistance to enable the new government to give a measure of service equal to that which people are*

going to expect. We may not all agree with the fundamentals of social credit, but we can hope that time will tell, or show, what social credit will do for Alberta.

–Nanton News, August 29, 1934

But even at the start, Aberhart had difficulties. None of the new Social Credit MLAs had any government experience. Even though they adapted to the legislature and sat as MLAs and cabinet ministers until the sweep of Peter Lougheed's Progressive Conservative Party in 1971, their early steps were stumbles.

Implementing many of the Social Credit ideals in the proper legislation proved difficult. Considering the state of Alberta's economy and the coffers of the provincial government, Alberta could not offer $25 a month for every citizen of the province. The province defaulted on $3.2 million worth of bonds and, in the summer of 1936, employed one of its most unusual schemes.

The Hon. Lucian Maynard as the main speaker, supported by Premier Aberhart, explained to a large audience of Calgary businessmen on Wednesday night last, the proposed issuing of "Prosperity Certificates" and what his hope by the government will be accomplished when these certificates are given circulation. The minister answered a large number of questions which had been asked and stated that he did not know so many questions could be asked on a subject which is "quite clear to me."

From what can be gathered from newspaper reports of the meeting, the government proposes in the first place to create a reserve of "real money" to cash the certificates that may be turned into the treasury thought wholesale and business house in need of "cash" to pay for outside of province commitments. The minister stated that the province would use extreme caution in issuing of the certificates so that the fund would always be in a liquid condition. If this can be done, and the people of the province become convinced of their value as a secondary circulating medium, all will be well, but if the reverse should be the case, the province will be in a sorry predicament.

Each week the holder will have to place a one cent stamp on each dollar, this stamp to be purchased from the provincial government with "real money." When 104 stamps are affixed, the certificate can be cashed. The great game will be to pass them on as fast as possible to avoid the stamp penalty and this in itself, to a certain extent, stimulate business, providing the certificates are generally accepted by the public as being "good money."

The experiment will be watched with keen interest. It would seem that the success or failure of the scheme will rest with the business men of the province into whose hands they will come very shortly after they have been issued. If business men will not, or cannot, accept as being face value, then the whole structure will tumble to earth and go down in provincial history as a foolish experiment.

–*Banff Crag and Canyon,* June 19, 1936

As predicted, the scheme did fail, partly because Albertans did not accept this new money and also because the Supreme Court of Canada deemed that Aberhart's prosperity certificates were not legal tender. In fact, the Supreme Court ruled that many of the Acts the SoCreds passed in their first years in power were "ultra-vires," or beyond the powers of provincial government.

The earlier calls by the weekly newspapers for patience for the new government quickly disappeared, and support for the government began to wane. One of Aberhart's successful policies to become legislation was the Recall Act, passed in 1936 and allowing constituents of a riding to launch an effort to recall their MLA and force him to resign. Ironically,

Prosperity Certificate issued by the Social Credit Party, 1936

Aberhart was the first politician subjected to his own legislation, becoming the only politician in Canadian history to be subject to a recall. In 1937, two-thirds of constituents of his Okotoks/High River riding signed a petition calling for his recall. The local paper supported the move and went one step further.

> If Premier Aberhart should resign, and the prospect does not seem remote, his government should resign with him. Alberta should write "finis" to its Social Credit experiment and start out on a new line of business government.
>
> It is only fair that Social Credit should have had its chance. The majority of the electors sincerely believed that it might work. But if they could have foreseen that the people were to be led into blind alleys, the futile bypaths of the last eighteen months, they would not have voted as they did. It is time they had a chance to record another vote. They expected, and with perfect right, that Social Credit be put into effect. Never

*was a government given fuller opportunity to make good and
never has a government failed more disastrously.*

–High River Times, March 25, 1937

Aberhart's government, however, immediately repealed their own
Recall Act, declaring all recall proceedings null and void, and denying
the High River/Okotoks group a refund of the $200 they were required
to pay to begin recall proceedings. In an article in the *High River Times*,
Aberhart stated, "I am not going to tender my resignation to any little
group in a hotel room. If anything is done, it will have to be done on the
floor of the legislature so that people know who is responsible."

For months, Aberhart and members of his party engaged in a battle
of words with Alberta's newspapers. "The school, the banks, the newspapers and such institutions should function for the benefit of the people,"
MLA Edith Gostick declared in the *High River Times* on September 2,
1937. "But we have reporters and editors who are paid for misinforming
the public. It is their means of livelihood. I had not thought that the *High
River Times* was amongst the financially owned and controlled press but
I guess it must be."

The High River Times replied a week later.

> *Mrs. Gostick's assumption that all newspapers not support-
> ing Social Credit must be the tool of financial interests is too
> ridiculous to be considered seriously even by the most credu-
> lous, though it may serve as an argument for government
> oppressed. As the* New Age *[the UK weekly in which the
> Social Credit theories were first published] blandly puts it:
> "there is no reason why the government should allow news-
> papers to behave with the same freedom as to the methods
> of influencing opinion as they have behave in the past. In
> fact those newspapers, insofar as they speak to the citizens
> of Alberta, on behold of sectional interest in Alberta, should
> voluntarily rally to the support of the Albertan government."*

And when this is achieved, when all the newspapers fall on their faces and cry with one voice, the glory and omnipotence of the Aberhart government, will the con be purged of any dissenting element. There will still be freedom of the press to be suppressed. The pulpits, the schools, the radio, the street corner conversation must be whipped into line. Spies must stationed everywhere to expose or punish any work or opinion lacking the required warmth and adulation. No more can communities meet in the free spontaneity of the past. Everywhere will be spies and a period of terror and distrust can be created, such as no Anglo-Saxon people have ever conceived.

–High River Times, September 9, 1937

Aberhart himself believed that save for one or two exceptions, journalists were irresponsible drunks and puppets of the banks. "The press tears down the pathway of life, not caring whose name may be maligned. Why pay 35 cents a week to those who oppose any benefit to the people," he stated later on. "We license doctors, we license lawyers, and school teachers and businessmen and auto drivers and hotel keepers for the protection of the public; why shouldn't the newspapers be licensed also."

In response to these licensing threats, the Alberta division of the Canadian Weekly Newspapers Association in its September 25, 1937, newsletter, urged every single member to attend the annual convention slated for October 8 and 9 in Edmonton. "Reasons for this threat are quite evident," it said in Bulletin Number 25.

The majority of Alberta newspapers have not been in sympathy with the present administration.

This free expression of opinion and the warnings published during the past two or three years have been fully vindicated by the absolute failure of extravagant promises made in the name of Social Credit. Though the majority of the people heeded not the warning, it is to the credit of the Alberta Press that subsequent events have justified their editorial opinions and their endeavor to keep the people honestly informed. The newspapers must, henceforth, attempt to safeguard their own interests and defend their rights with more vigor than has ever before been displayed.

Despite the howls of outrage, Aberhart made good on his threat, passing the Accurate News and Information Act on October 1, 1937. The new act established a Social Credit Board to oversee the operations of Alberta newspapers and required all newspapers to be licensed by the provincial government. It also made it mandatory for all newspapers to publish, without any financial compensation, any statement issued on the policy and activity of the Social Credit Board. Furthermore, if the board was interested in a piece that had appeared in any newspaper in the province, an article or an editorial, they could demand that the newspaper submit the names, addresses and occupations of all the sources and staffers involved in the development of the piece. Finally, the provincial cabinet, upon recommendation of the board, could suspend the publication of any newspaper in the province, for any reason and for any length of time.

Across the province, editorial after editorial declared their outrage in Aberhart's efforts to control and muzzle the press. Comparisons to fascist states in Germany and Italy were not uncommon.

A dictatorship in Canada can hardly be imagined; yet, when we see how Huey Long established a dictatorship in Louisiana in spite of the constitution of the United States, we cannot be sure of the protection of the B.N.A. Act the British traditions of constitutional government.

That the freedom of the press is frequently abused none would deny. Nevertheless, the laws provide protection from such abuses. Canadian libels laws are strict, and obscenity is punishable. It does not seem necessary to adopt the methods of Hitler and Mussolini anyplace in Canada.

–Nanton News, September 17, 1936

This is the class of political party Alberta has in control of its affairs today and this is the party which would deny the press the liberty is has enjoyed for centuries and the employees of the banks the rights of every citizen. Is there anything in Alberta that the Aberhart government has overlooked while grinding down the common people into the dust. Now bring all this right home to Drumheller, the Review *asks Herbert Ingery, of Wayne, Social credit member for the Drumheller Constituency in the Alberta legislature: "What have you been doing while all this has been going on?" What have you got to say Mr. Ingrey? You are the representative of some 4500 Alberta voters and they will not stand for such things. You have gone pillar to post in this constituency loudly proclaiming that you were fighting the cause of the common people, while things are infinitely worse for the people in this constituency. You have drawn indemnity with consistent regularity and have evidently been quite content to play the part of a human rubber stamp for the Aberhart Government. Right or wrong it has been your government. But the handwriting is on the wall and while social credit members will hang on until the last dog is hung, to use an old expression, the social credit jig is up. The longer the government hangs on, the greater the deluge of defeat.*

Meanwhile, think it over dear readers, and become outspoken in your allegiance to the fastest growing arm. Alberta has seen those who are rebelling against the tyrannical acts of a dictatorial and disloyal government.

–Drumheller Review, October 7, 1937

Even supporters of Aberhart, such as the *Sedgewick Community Press,* found fault with the new Press Act.

> *Mr. Aberhart uses the figure of speech that if obstacles are encountered in a piece of farm land plough around them. Well, we don't use plows in a printing office, be we have pounded linotype keyboard ever since Mergenthaler invented the great machine that keeps the world informed, and regardless of the fact that I personally backed the Social Credit program from its inception in Alberta, it might be well for Mr. Aberhart to reflect back to the summer preceding the 1935 election and note no political party or government ever deigned to suggest that the Press of the Province should be so controlled as to make it mandatory for the publishers to give away for any purpose whatsoever.*
>
> *If the above statements have the earmarks of defiance, it is only necessary to utilize some of the phraseology employed by the learned Premier, who has often alluded to the fact that what, therefore a man sows that also she be reap.*

> –*Sedgewick Community Press,* October 7, 1937

In a show of solidarity not seen since the early days of the Alberta Press Association, every daily and weekly newspaper in the province banded together to fight the Social Credit attempt to destroy free press in Alberta. As a group, newspapers across the province took the Aberhart government to court to fight the Accurate News and Information Act. When the case reached the Supreme Court of Canada, it attracted attention and news media from around the world.

Reporters from venerable American newspapers, such as the *New York Times* and the *Chicago Tribune,* descended upon Edmonton to cover the legislature. On March 4, 1938, the Supreme Court ruled that the Accurate News and Information Act was unconstitutional, and it was tossed out, ending one of the most fascinating battles for the free press ever seen in North America.

The fight for the freedom of the press in Alberta did not go unnoticed. For many years it has been reported that on May 2, 1938, the *Edmonton Journal* became the first media outlet outside the United States to receive a special citation of the Pulitzer Prize for its commendable efforts in the fight against Aberhart and his Accurate News Act. But forgotten is that a large number of Alberta weeklies (and the rest of the other dailies for that matter) also received special citations from the Pulitzer committee for their efforts in the free press battle. Every paper that had signed on to the battle, including the 80 members of the Alberta Weekly Newspapers Association, received a certificate that read:

> *The Trustees of Columbia University*
> *in the City of New York*
> *To all person to whom these presents may come greeting*
> *Be it known that*
> [the newspaper's name was inserted here]
> *Has been awarded recognition for its cooperation with the Edmonton Journal, recipient of a special Pulitzer Prize for distinguished and meritorious public service in 1937 in accordance with the provisions of the Statutes of the University Governing such award*
>
> *In witness whereof we have caused this diploma to be signed by the President of the University and our Corporate Seal to be hereto affixed in the City of New York on the First Day of June in the year of our Lord one thousand nine hundred and thirty eight.*

"It's a tribute to the courage of the publishers of the Alberta weeklies," said Pat Brennan, a professor of history at the University of Calgary in an article printed in the *Macleod Gazette*. "They were more dependent on the government revenue from advertising than the dailies. Readers were bigger supporters of Social Credit than those in Calgary and Edmonton.

But weeklies took the position that this is a free country and they would not support this act. They took the moral high road."

But public interest in the war between Aberhart and Alberta newspapers quickly faded. Despite a drop in popularity, Aberhart and the Social Credit won the 1940 provincial election. In the southern regions of Alberta, though, some citizens were dabbling in communism.

⁓

CHAPTER ELEVEN

Blairmore and the "Reds"

MORE THAN ONE BATTLE BETWEEN elected officials and newspapers was occurring in Alberta during the mid-1930s. In Blairmore, the local newspaper took on a foe that 20 years later would be the scourge of the Western world: communism.

Located in the heart of coal country and hit hard by the numerous closures of coalmines in the area, Blairmore suffered considerably during the Great Depression. And like other industrial municipalities in Canada, many town residents had deep connections with labour unions. In 1933, that bond resulted in the election of a town council and school board completely made up of members of the Communist Party of Canada, including Bill Knight as mayor.

The "communist" council took more of a populist approach in their efforts by reducing utility charges and taxes on homes. They also allowed people to grow food on all unused public lands and built a shelter for many of the area's residents as well as workers made homeless by the Depression.

At the same time, the school board ordered that students would no longer mark Remembrance Day because it was an "imperialist" holiday and would instead celebrate the May 1 holiday to honour the Russian

Revolution in 1917. The council immediately fired the police and fire chiefs and the town electrician, and passed a motion asking the federal government to remove the official in charge of the local customs house.

The council also changed the name of Blairmore's main street, Victoria Avenue, to Tim Buck Avenue, after the imprisoned leader of the Communist Party of Canada (the original name was later reinstated).

What an insult!

Canadian citizens have been subjected to indignities unparalleled in a supposedly democratic and liberty-loving community. Well might people throughout the province and the Dominion wonder why such conditions should prevail.

The only answer is that a majority of the ratepayers voted for a council and school board avowedly anti-British, dominated by a Communist agitator who has not one vestige on interest in the Crows' Nest Pass. People living outside of Blairmore are perplexed, not knowing the cosmopolitan nature of its population and how susceptible it is to irresponsible leadership.

It is amazing that such thing should happen, and it is high time that the people of Blairmore, who prize Canadian ideals of citizenship, assert themselves and redeem the good name of their town in the eyes of Canada. It can be done—not by a milk and water attitude, by showing they are in possession of sufficient spirit to uphold the principles of Canadian citizenship against the encroachment of a clique who would meet a speedy termination to similar activities were they to practice them in the country they hold up as a pattern to the people of Blairmore.

–Coleman Journal, date unknown, 1933

Tim Buck, leader of the Communist Party of Canada, visiting Blairmore, ca. 1935

The editorial in the *Coleman Journal* was reprinted in the *Blairmore Enterprise*, a weekly published and edited by William James Bartlett who was born in 1880 in Curling, which was in the British colony of Newfoundland. He came west in 1907, first to Coleman and later to Blairmore, where in 1910 he became a partner in the *Enterprise* with J.D.S. Barrett, a fellow Newfoundlander who had founded the paper in 1909. The partnership owned four newspapers: the *Enterprise*, the *Bellevue Times,* the *Cowley Chronicle and Lundbreck Advertiser* and the *Frank Vindicator*. By time the communists came to power in Blairmore, Barrett had dissolved the partnership and moved to the West Coast. He passed away in 1929.

In response to the reprinted editorial, along with other critical editorials in the *Blairmore Enterprise*, Mayor Knight ordered that the town's annual statement, which was usually printed by the *Enterprise* and its journeymen printers, to be typed and duplicated by town workers. But despite opposition from the local press, Knight, the communist council and the school board were, in the 1934 election, re-elected or declared elected by acclamation. The local paper cried foul in how the election was run.

> *Property owners, who have resided in Blairmore for upwards of twenty-five years, and paid taxes, promptly during all that time, were refused the privilege of voting at Monday's elections, while many others with not a cent invested in the district voted, and without question.*
>
> *–Blairmore Enterprise, February 15, 1934*

In 1935, however, the communist coalition began to fall apart. The man they appointed police chief was charged with extortion and theft, a story not only covered by the local press, but it was front-page news across Canada. Bill Knight had been invited by the Communist Party of Canada to speak in Toronto, and he expensed the trip to the town. And many other financial irregularities or concerns were laid out in the town's annual auditor's report.

> *Take, for instance, the item of election expenses ($246.30)— the biggest ever known in the town of Blairmore; dog taxes ($49.00)—the amount claimed to have been paid for tags for the year, not representing the 30% of the dogs allowed to prowl around town; legal expenses ($760.40) the biggest in the town's history; delegates' expenses ($459.00), which included Mayor Knight's trip to Toronto on other than town's business. What charge in this connection could be laid is difficult to say, but it amounted to "money taken from the treasury for an illegal purpose." It is not intended for such purpose, and the mayor and the others who signed the cheque must know so.*
>
> *There are but a few of the most glaring items suggested through the auditor's report. How does the $9376.11 compare*

with the deficit estimated a few months ago of around $4000.00
for the year 1935?

–*Blairmore Enterprise*, January 24, 1936

In light of these scandals, none of the incumbent councillors and school board members stood in the next municipal election. Many of their policies around taxation, school holidays and street names were overturned.

The *Blairmore Enterprise* continued under the guidance of William Bartlett until his death on May 16, 1946. The paper barely lasted two more months more, publishing its final edition on July 26.

~

Mercury
The Tofield

www.tofieldmerc.com   twitter.com/tofieldmercury

The *Tofield Mercury* has served the Tofield, Ryley and Holden areas in Beaver County since 1917, as well as the hundreds of acreage residents west of Tofield.

The newspaper was first established as the *Tofield Standard*, until 1918 when William Worton, from Yarmouth, England, purchased the paper and renamed it the *Mercury* after his hometown paper.

In the early 1960s, the *Tofield Mercury* was owned by Chuck MacLean, who also published the *Camrose Canadian*. He owned the *Mercury* until 1985 when his daughter Anne Francoeur took over and ran the paper until March 1999, at which time Kerry Anderson, Rick Truss and partners purchased it.

The new owners also published *The Community Press* out of Sedgewick and the *Viking Weekly Review*. They later started up the monthly advertiser, *East Central Times,* and in October 2005 opened up the *Lamont Leader*. Kerry Anderson became the sole owner of the paper in 2006 when Rick Truss retired from publishing.

Over the years, the *Mercury* has gone from hand-fed type to now having the most modern of computer equipment and publishing programs.

The *Tofield Mercury* has won numerous awards over the years, including a top editorial prize and a Blue Ribbon Award, ranking it in general excellence among the top newspapers in Canada for its circulation.

The *Mercury* has also been a community leader by spearheading fundraising drives for Manitoba flood victims, Kosovo refugees, tsunami aid and Hurricane Katrina relief.

CHAPTER TWELVE

World War II

O N SEPTEMBER 1, 1939, NAZI-CONTROLLED Germany invaded Poland. The same day, France, Britain and the Commonwealth countries, including Canada, declared war on Germany. Once again, the world was at war, and with the Japanese attacking Pearl Harbor in 1941, there were two major fronts. Six years passed before peace reigned.

However, the rumours of war, the rattling of sabres, had been ongoing for years before the official declarations of war in 1939. Hitler and his Nazis had been "annexing" various parts of Europe, Japan had invaded China, and throughout the world, people were preparing for war. At the same time, it was hoped that horrors of war could be diverted.

Whatever immediate danger an outburst of war might offer, it should be the ardent hope of every sane man and woman that it be averted. War has done more to damn the human race than all other human perversities. In spite of its glorification by historic propaganda, patriotic emotionalism, and racial egotism, war is hell. It was cruel and barbarous when warrior faced warrior with drawn sword pitting strength, courage and skill in individual combat. Then there was at least the thrill of contest—a test of prowess. Now, war is an abomination, a scourge, a wholesale murder, in which men

bleed and die in shambles without a chance to defend them-
selves. From the restrictions of the battlefield, war has spread
until it is a butchery of innocents in towns and cities, far
removed from the battle lines. War has become so terrible
so positively inhuman, so frightfully devastating, that every
intelligent man and woman should hold it in horror and dis-
gust. When that attitude against war has become universal,
the warlords will have to fight it out between themselves and
that will mean the end of war.

–*Cardston News*, February 2, 1937

The actions of Hitler, and later the Japanese, made it impossible for
war to be disregarded, so Canada and Alberta responded to this war in the
same way they did to World War I, with patriotism, honour and service.

The fateful hour against which all men of peace and good will
have prayed and devoutly hoped has struck. Great Britain,
and with her the British Empire, is at war with the black force
of Hitlerism—force which if they had their way would change
the world from what is desired by all who believe in inter-
national law and order to a world in which the principle of
violence will be dominant. The arch-enemy of all that demo-
cratic nations hold dear has thrown down the challenge of
war and it has been taken up by Great Britain and France
as the guardians of peace and liberty which the Fuehrer of
Germany has sought to destroy. However desirous of peace no
other step could have been taken. The challenge is a challenge
to humanity, a challenge to civilized law and order, a chal-
lenge to the survival of those free institutions which have been
built up by the democracies of the world.

It is a war in which the issue is whether the law of violence,
the law of brute force, shall establish itself and take place of
ordered government to which the world has advanced has
brought about. The forces of light are arrayed against the

Leonard C. Newsome of the *Chronicle*, Crossfield, 1911

forces of darkness, denoted in Hitlerism—a monster which has to be crushed if peace is to flourish, allowing nations and individuals to live their lives in security, freed from an ever-present menace. It is a war of humanity against inhumanity with inhumanity provoking it and calling for it.

To the last man and the last dollar!

–Stavely Advertiser, September 8, 1939

During the six years of the war, over 85,000 men enlisted, including people involved in Alberta's weekly newspaper industry.

The editor of the *Big Valley News*, A.E. Ellison, enlisted in the RCAF, as did George Wheeler, the son of *Acme Sentinel* publisher and founder, Arthur Wheeler; Herbert Campbell Ford, son of *Lacombe Globe* publisher Harry Ford; and Leonard Newsome, father of Ronnie Newsom,

G. Gordon of the *Herald*, Ponoka, 1911

a long-time weekly journalist who had worked for several newspapers in Alberta. Four years before his enlistment, Ronnie had been working under William Henry Miller, the publisher of the *Olds Gazette*.

Many other newspaper owners also answered the call and enlisted. John Gordon's family had owned the *Ponoka Herald* since 1905. His father George "Scotty" Gordon not only ran the *Herald* until his death in 1938, but he had also been that town's postmaster for 26 years. John Gordon had worked in the banking industry but returned to run the paper after his father's death.

When war broke out, John enlisted and served in the RAF. Gordon was almost 40 at the time, and he was different from most of the Alberta newspapermen who enlisted in World War II because he had also served in World War I. After the war, he returned to Ponoka and ran the *Herald* until 1953, selling the paper to a three-way partnership that included Keith Leonard, Ernie Jamison and Ken McLean. Leonard passed away less than a year later, and the partnership of Jamison and McLean continued running the paper until 1964, when McLean assumed sole ownership. McLean ran the *Herald* at least until 1982. Jamison finally ended up owning the *St. Albert Gazette*.

Another interesting "newspaperman" who enlisted in the war was the son of a United Church minister in Bon Accord. In the mid-1930s, Eddie Arrol was the publisher and editor of the *Bon Accord Herald*, the first and only newspaper ever produced in that town. He was only 12 years old when he began his first venture into publishing and published the paper for only three years. During the war, Arrol served in the RCAF and afterwards published the short-lived *Redwater Herald* before moving to Calgary to become a photographer.

The newspaper editors, publishers, reporters, printers and other employees who enlisted to fight in World War II did so voluntarily because they were exempt from any conscription. During the war, the government had designated newspapers to be an essential service.

"It is my firm belief that the first duty of every newspaper in Canada is to direct public and private opinion to the successful prosecution of Canada's part in the British Commonwealth War effort," declared R.L. King (publisher of the *Claresholm Local Press* and president of the Alberta branch of the Canadian Weekly Newspapers Association) at the 1941 convention in Edmonton. "There are forces at work that would inject fear and doubt into the hearts of our people…it is all the more reason for constant vigilance and a never-ending fight to combat an influence that would divide our war effort or that menaces our society from without or within."

SERVING LAMONT COUNTY

Read us online at www.lamontleader.com
twitter.com/lamontleader

Publisher of *The Community Press*, *Viking Weekly Review*, *Tofield Mercury*, *Beaver County Chronicle* and *East Central Times*, Kerry Anderson started up the *Lamont Leader* on October 3, 2005. The newspaper joined the Alberta Weekly Newspapers Association in 2008 as well as the Canadian Community Newspapers Association (CCNA).

The *Lamont Leader* covers the news for rural and urban residents of Lamont County, with 4200 papers circulated free each week. The newspaper can also be read online (lamontleader.com).

Since the paper began in 2005, its revenue has continued to grow as the paper established itself as the main publication in Lamont County and the only weekly paper with an office within the county.

In a short time, the *Lamont Leader* has already won best historical feature story in Canada through the CCNA for its spread on the 50th anniversary of the train/bus collision at Lamont that killed numerous school children, mostly from the Chipman area.

The *Lamont Leader* is distributed in, and covers news from, Bruderheim, Lamont, Andrew, Mundare, Chipman, Star, St. Michael and Hilliard—all communities within Lamont County.

As with the Great War 25 years earlier, Alberta weeklies varied in their coverage of the war. Some featured weekly articles and editorials on the events and battles overseas, while others kept such articles to a minimum and focused, in typical weekly fashion, on local events and/or incidents relating to the populace. Still, no matter how much war news was published in a weekly, none of these weeklies ever shirked its duty to provide its readership with local news.

Next to stories about the disaster of Dunkirk, the bombing of Pearl Harbor, the invasion at Normandy and the celebrations of V-E and V-J Days were the accounts of the most recent Woman's Institute meeting, the reports from the surrounding towns, the names of the winners at the local fair, the development of the new school, the town council notes and all the other fundamental information usually present in a weekly newspaper.

> When a world war is raging and history is being made every day in the week, [weekly newspapers] follow the even tenor of their way and continue to report the short and simple annals of the common people who do not make history but only life. Their function is not to give the world news but community news, not to publish the mere superficial facts, but to maintain and build up the old time atmosphere of a free democratic country which is in danger of being lost and forgotten in our new social order.
>
> –Stettler Independent, 1941

But on the whole, Alberta newspapers responded to World War II in the same way they did to World War I.

"Now, when our country is at war, our duties are more pressing and important than ever," said Canadian Weekly Newspapers Association (CWNA) president Len D'Albertanson at the organization's 1942 convention. "On our shoulders falls part of the onus of welding rural Canada into a unified fighting nation. A lukewarm public spirit which is apt to

Len D'Albertanson (left) and Charles Clark, 1947, Edmonton

forget and fail to appreciate the realities of this terrible conflict…must be whipped up."

In response to these calls and to support their local communities and the country as a whole, Alberta weeklies wrote highly patriotic editorials and published letters from soldiers overseas. The papers noted promotions and postings of local soldiers and prominently, but respectfully, featured stories about the soldiers killed in action. Despite these tragic occurrences, Alberta weeklies were beacons of optimism, even during times of extreme heartbreak and hopelessness and even when the fate of a small town was in question.

On Monday, August 24, 1942, dawned the darkest day for Stettler and the surrounding district which we can recollect in our long experience here.

Since news was received on Wednesday that tanks had landed at Dieppe to spearhead the extensive commando attack and that the Calgary Tank Regiment had covered itself with glory, word has been anxiously awaited by relatives and friends here. As the day passed with no word of casualties, hope grew. Perhaps the Company of the Calgary Regiment which was so largely made up from the District was among those who had been prevented from landing. Vain hope indeed. Early Monday morning telegraph messages to relatives began to trickle through. Before noon the trickle had become a torrent and word received that many of the local boys were missing. Gloom spread and settled over the district like a pall as name after name was added to the growing list.

Out of the shock and gloom of the first news comes the bright stories of their valor and courage; and we know that all who took part in the that action acquitted themselves well and have brought naught but valor to the names of their families, their native land and this small town and district. When, indeed, "shall their glory fade"?

–*Stettler Independent*, August 26, 1942

On August 19, about 6000 Allied troops, most of them Canadians, had participated in the raid on Dieppe. Historically, the goals of the attack were to hold a major port in continental Europe for a short period of time, to test German responses and to gather intelligence. The plan failed, and more than half of the soldiers who made it ashore were captured, killed or taken prisoner. More than 100 of these POWs were from central Alberta, serving in the 14th Canadian Army Tank Regiment, also known as the Calgary Tanks.

And the 14th Company, which formed the centre of the Calgary Tanks, was made up of boys from twenty years of age and upwards, who had never seen battle before, and who were pitted against the veterans of the German Occupation Army, with all their fortifications in front of them.

They had nothing except a few months training in England. They were recruited in Stettler and the neighbouring towns a year and a half ago, and were taken from the farms, and the stores, and the schools without ever handling a gun. Yet they helped put to rout the most disciplined army in Europe, rounded up Nazi prisoners; and some of them died in Dieppe's narrow streets.

The casualties were heavy in proportion to their numbers, if we count as casualties those who were killed, wounded and prisoners of war. Out of 7 recruits, Gadsby had five reported missing. Out of 38, Stettler had 24 reported missing. Out of 6, Erskine had 4 reported missing. Out of 15, Castor had 7 missing. It may be that many of those reported missing will later on be discovered as prisoners of war or will escape from the soil of France. Those who have lost their sons for the time being, should not lose hope because the hazards of war are in their favour.

But if in the weeks to come, some of them are reported as "Probably Dead" we have the consolation that they performed their duty to the supreme limit.

–Stettler Independent, September 2, 1942

Other stories of tragedies during the war were reported, but there were also stories of valour. Canada and Alberta suffered several losses, but in 1943 and 1944, the tide seemed to be turning. The Allies were gaining ground on the Axis, and though many hard battles still had to be fought, people began to look to the future, when the war would be over.

During the 1944 CWNA convention, Alberta president W.H. Schier-hotlz of the *Rocky Mountain House News* said, "After victory on the battlefields is won, we have a no less important issue to face, one which we as publishers cannot evade and must not shirk. The return to civilian life of hundreds of thousands now in the armed forces and in war industries will present problems which will require clear thinking, deep sympathy and tolerant understanding."

And when the war in Europe ended in April 1945 (the Japanese surrendered in August), celebrations took place in the streets of almost every town in Alberta. At the same time of this joy, there was awareness that the battle was not yet finished.

Experience has shown that many of the ills which in the past have befallen this country and the world at large have been the result of our failure to foresee certain eventualities, and to plan for them. Canada, in coming with many other nations, has had the misfortune to experience two wars, and a depression of unprecedented proportions, within the last twenty years.

As a result, there has been a united opinion among the people of Canada in favor of a plan for dealing with the inevitable difficulties of the post-war period, and especially in regard to providing for those who will be discharged from the services. In looking back over events which followed the first world war, it has been realized that many of the problems which developed then, could be avoided a second time. With the purpose in view, a great deal of study has been devoted to plans for Post-War Reconstruction in Canada

–Picture Butte Progress, date unknown, 1945

We along with the Allied world, rejoice in the Victory in Europe and give thanks to God for the end of the conflict there. We also have two great hopes, the first being the unconditional surrender of Japan will come in the near future, and the other is that the world may have Peace as well as Victory.

The Allied nations have had to join together in the fight for Victory, they will also have to join in the struggle for peace. A peace that will be lasting.

Each of us has an individual and joint task in bringing this Peace about. It will be no good looking to the Government, any government, to alone bring about permanent Peace, we must all work and pray for such a blessing.

It is so easy to leave it to the other fellow, put him in office and say "go to it". With the very best of intentions anyone will find it very difficult to carry out plans for the betterment of the country without the whole-hearted support of those who put him in office.

In the world of tomorrow, that world for which such great hopes are held, let us all do our share to bring about those things we all want, Peace and Security.

–Taber Times, May 10, 1945

CHAPTER THIRTEEN

Enemy Aliens

WHEN WALTER KOYANAGI CAME TO the Taber area, he was not welcomed with open arms. Koyanagi, who was born just outside of Vancouver, on Sea Island, now the location of the Vancouver International Airport, was of Japanese descent. Despite his Canadian birth, he was, like most Japanese Canadians, declared an "enemy alien" immediately following the bombing of Pearl Harbor in 1941.

A large number of Japanese Canadians were stripped of their land and their businesses and sent to internment camps, some of which were located in Alberta. With so many men gone off to serve on the front lines, there was a labour shortage in the agricultural industries, and the use of enemy aliens was seen as a practical solution to this problem. In 1942, Koyanagi and his family worked in the southern Alberta sugar beet fields during the war.

But the locals in Taber were not happy with the arrival of the Koyanagis and other Japanese Canadians. For a good part of 1942, the *Taber Times* ran several editorials and articles strongly opposing the relocation of these Japanese enemy aliens to the Taber area.

> *A horrified world heard and read Wednesday reports of the atrocities committed by the Japanese at Hong Kong and*

Taber Times building, undated

resolved to offer no quarter to the Japs, but fight on with every means possible to rid the world of all time of such fiends.

For long years the Japanese have been a great problem in British Columbia and now these districts are being faced with a similar threat. Do you, the people of Taber and districts want an influx of Japanese in these districts? To lower the standards of living—to be a national problem in times of strife and to usurp the opportunities of our boys who are offering their lives to fight for each of us and to save us from such atrocities as have been committed in Hong Kong?

Can we who pride ourselves as being true citizens of this Great Dominion of Canada, look on the atrocities of Hong Kong and the proven treachery and low standard of living of these Japs and still want to bring them into our midst?

Sugar is sweet—and so is life sweet—but our boys are offering their all for our way of life—can we think the sweetness of sugar the greater value.

Arthur Avery of *Taber Times* at printing press, undated

Surely we can find ways to harvest our sugar crops without inviting the Japs to live in our midst. For of a certainty they will stay here if once brought in, and after the war we will be forced with a large population of Japs that will hang as millstones around our guilty necks, the necks of our children, in just retribution to our lack of ability, our laziness or our greed in bringing them in.

–Taber Times, March 12, 1942

The *Taber Times* wasn't the only newspaper concerned about enemy aliens, and the views of Arthur H. Avery, who had been the publisher/editor of the *Times* since 1927, weren't unusual. In fact, it was in tune with the opinion of the times. Many suspected that Japanese Canadians, even those who had been born in Canada, and some of those who had fought for Canada in World War I, could be enemy aliens. And it wasn't only the Japanese who were suspect. Many German Canadians, Chinese Canadians and even some First Nation peoples who had "Asian features," were considered possible enemy aliens and placed in internment camps.

But the situation with the long-running newspaper in Taber and Japanese enemy aliens would, in time, become a more interesting story.

> Before the Japanese were brought into these districts we published an Editorial entitled, "Shall we cast away our heritage?" Judging by the reaction of some of our citizens, this Editorial caused uneasiness in the breasts of many. One of the points was that "of certainty they will stay here if once brought in."

> Well, as the saying goes "they came, they saw, they conquered"— and don't be fooled, the Japanese are right now doing a pretty thorough job of conquering right here in Taber. They came for beet work, then it was the Cannery, next will be working in homes throughout the town and country—and then what?

> Complacency and shutting our eyes to facts just won't accomplish anything, unless some drastic action is taken our fears will materialize and Taber and district will be faced with a large population of Japanese after the war.

> Some say the Japanese will be moved out of our district after the war—where to?—B.C. certainly won't take them.
>
> –*Taber Times*, September 17, 1942

Avery was correct about one thing in his editorial: many Japanese did stay in the Taber area after the war, including Walter Koyanagi. Since his family had nothing left back on the West Coast, Koyanagi says they had no choice but to stay. But not long after the war, in 1950, he got a job at the *Taber Times,* working for Arthur Avery, the same man who had demonized Japanese enemy aliens during his wartime editorials.

"Like in all small town newspapers, I did everything that needed to get done," Koyanagi says in an interview for this book. "I worked in

Jack Gieg (left) and Walter Koyanagi (*Taber Times*), in late 1970s

the back shop, running the Linotype and as an all around handy man and printer, I worked in the front as an accountant. I did everything you could think of."

In 1966, Avery sold the paper to George Meyer, a Bow Island native who at various times after the war had been a partner or owner in a number of Alberta papers, including the *Camrose Canadian,* the *Tofield Mercury* and the *Nanton News.* Koyanagi remained as an employee at the *Taber Times* until 1970.

In his book, *A Prairie Publisher,* George Meyer claimed that he had a nightmare in which Koyanagi said he was leaving the *Times* to start his own accountant business in town. Meyer was worried that he would be losing one of his best employees, so the next day Meyer offered Koyanagi a chance to become a partner in the *Taber Times.*

George Meyer, 1950s

In October 1970, the former "enemy alien" became a partner in the *Taber Times*, a paper that had at one time painted people of his descent as treacherous and a threat to the way of life in Taber. Koyanagi and Meyer were partners in the *Times* for almost a decade and were key in switching the paper from a sheet-fed offset press with a new web offset press, the first Alberta newspaper south of Calgary to do so. Because of this change, they started printing other newspapers, and over time, were printing almost every community newspaper in southern Alberta. The partnership also bought the *Coaldale Sunny South News* and founded the *Vauxhall Advance* in 1978. They sold the entire operation in 1983. Walter Koyanagi, at age 89 in 2009, still lived in the Taber area.

Newspaperman John M. Bender established the *Nanton News* on June 25, 1903, which, interestingly, was one week after the village of Nanton was incorporated. Bender's intention from day one was the same as any other pioneer newspaperman of the day— to help the country grow. His vision of Nanton was of steady growth in the business district to correspond with the increasing population of the entire area.

Bender realized that the best way to give the settlers and businessmen information was to start a newspaper in Nanton. This encouraged trade and the exchange of information between people living in the town. The *News* kept its readers apprised of current events as well as available goods and services. Don't forget that it was the readers and advertisers who kept the *News* in business from its beginnings, until today.

Early on, the advertisements were for building materials and the basics needed to survive on a homestead. This soon changed, however, to make room for the many advertised luxuries of the day, such as underwear that didn't shrink and window screens.

Aaron Z. Jessup bought the paper from Bender in May 1905. His son Clyde C. Jessup eventually became his partner, while his other son Ralph became a colleague in the newspaper business, publishing the *Macleod Gazette*. Clyde took over when the senior Jessup died in 1938. The *News* remained under his leadership until 1956, when the well-known George Meyer and Dick Hawk bought it.

In 1959, Meyer was the AWNA president who led a delegation to the provincial legislature, petitioning on behalf of weekly newspapers that provincial elections be held on a Monday to allow for timely local coverage. His quest was successful.

A.Z. Jessup of *Nanton News*, 1911

~

That same year, Meyer sold his shares in the *Nanton News* to Hawk, who continued to support commerce and growth in Nanton and the district as well as share interesting local colour items with the community, through current event coverage and columnists living in the area.

Hawk sold the paper in the 1980s to Ed and Lynn Maynard, who then sold it back to George Meyer in 1987. Meyer sold the *Nanton News* to Frank and Emily McTighe in September 1989. Frank and his wife sold the paper to Westmount Press in February 1995, although Frank remained the publisher of the *News* until April 1996. Bowes Publishers Ltd., a subsidiary of Sun Media, made the *Nanton News* part of a chain of weeklies and dailies when it purchased the *Nanton News* from Westmount Press in 1998.

Karen Freeman was appointed associate publisher from 1995

to 1999. Frank returned as publisher from October 1999 until September 2000. The *News*' current publisher, Nancy Middleton, succeeded Frank in September 2000.

As John Bender said in 1905, "Any person who induces people to town to trade is helping the entire business community, and no town is a success unless all lines of trade are working to extend business as far as possible, and trying to bring a larger territory in the circle of which the town is the business center."

Over the years, the *Nanton News*, along with all of its local colleagues, has done a good job of letting people know about town life and town news. The paper serves as a notice board for the community, announcing births, marriages and deaths, as well as yard sales, farm sales and farmers market dates. There have been some tough times though, such as when Nanton suffered with droughts and the BSE (bovine spongiform encephalopathy) crisis.

Looking toward more positive things, the *News* celebrated the successes of local folks who have shone through adversity and helped make our town a better place to live in.

The *News* continues to serve as the growing town's source of local information. Current events and availability of local goods are still part and parcel of what you'll find in its pages.

Some things haven't changed much in the 109 years of the *Nanton News*. The "old" families as well as the newcomers still look for the stories and pictures of their community, and everyone recognizes that the best way to advertise a new service or organization is by buying an ad in the paper.

As a long-standing member of the Alberta Weekly Newspapers Association, the *News* strives to live up to the AWNA mission, which is "to encourage, assist and ensure our members publish high quality community newspapers. The association achieves this by prioritizing education, marketing and fellowship."

The *News* has taken advantage of the education provided by the AWNA annual symposium and in the fellowship that those experiences provide it acknowledges the power of the blanket ad to generate revenue.

The partnership provided by the AWNA members is a tremendous advantage to everyone involved with the newspaper, including the readers. Whether they know AWNA is working on their behalf or not, the readers' experience of a weekly newspaper is enhanced by that work.

The *News* is one of the smaller weekly newspapers in the province, but its membership is no less valuable. Sharing the experiences of newspaper work with other members is a valuable and underestimated commodity that the paper offers.

CHAPTER FOURTEEN

Rumours of Oil

O N FEBRUARY 8, 1947, THE *Leduc Representative* ran a front-page article based on rumour. In operation for over 40 years—since February 22, 1907, to be exact—the paper was not known for running stories based on town rumours, especially on the front page.

Still, considering how the event mentioned in the story dramatically changed the history of Alberta, the coverage in the *Representative* was subdued, with a relatively small headline and placement to the side of the page. Based on the design of the page, it seemed that a boxed article about an essay contest for local students was the significant story of the week. Then again, the essay story might have been the most important article of that week because while many had hoped that an oil strike would have an impact on Alberta's economy, nobody was getting their hopes up. The feeling around oil strikes was positive, yet cautious.

> *Rumour of oil strikes, flowing wells, etc., were plentiful around Leduc early this week when it became known that Leduc No. 1, of the Imperial Oil Co., situated some 8 miles north west of Leduc, had been brought in.*
>
> *As this was written (Wednesday) very little definite information can be obtained on the subject. Any announcement,*

apparently, will have to come from the company's office at Calgary and this announcement is expected to be made in the near future.

–Leduc Representative, February 6, 1947

A proper announcement came a week later, with Imperial Oil hosting a major event, inviting hundreds to witness the "coming out" of Leduc Well No. 1. The occasion itself wasn't as spectacular as expected—it was February in Alberta, the weather was cold and it took longer for the oil to gush from the well. The planned "blowout" was scheduled for 10:00 AM, but Leduc No. 1 didn't "officially" begin flowing until 4:00 PM. By then, the crowd of several hundred who had originally gathered in the morning had dwindled down to less than 100.

Even so, the response to this event was slightly more celebrated in the next issue of the *Representative*—this time, the oil strike story was boxed in the top centre of the front page. Reaction, though, was still relatively cautious. The oil could bring an economic boom, but then again, it might not. Many other strikes in the province had not panned out to anything of significance because of the remoteness of the strike or the limited amount of oil expected. But if Leduc No. 1 did bring a much-welcomed economic boom, what form would it take and how would it change the circumstances of the community and shape its future?

Although that answer is now known, in the winter of 1947, nobody had any real idea of the implications of Leduc No. 1, only speculations.

What the future holds for this area is anyone's guess. Present prospects are that the Imperial concern has got something really good and intends to develop it, but even that is only a matter of conjecture until such time as the well is given a production test and the company announces its intentions in the matter. If the expected development does take place it may mean a great thing for the towns in this area and, to a less degree, the farming community as well. And right now is a good time for the towns and villages to make up their minds what they intend to do about it, if it does come. Already one school of thought has made its ideas on the subject all too plain. Stories of extortionate charges for everyday commodities are already in circulation around Leduc—possibly in other towns as well. There is an attitude evident on the part of some people to treat the drillers and other employees as necessary evils to be charged as much possible and given as little courtesy and service as we can get away with. Such an attitude will undoubtedly bring its own consequences to the economy of our districts. One or two disgruntled persons can give the towns more publicity (undesirable) than can be overcome by ten years of righteous dealings there-after.

So much for Leduc. What about Calmar, Thorsby, Breton, Warburg, etc.? The present strike does not by any means limit the exact field of future development. If experience in other fields is any criterion we may expect that further exploration to take place in all these towns and possibly more. Are they prepared for the increased of business. Can they handle an influx of ten or twenty families or more, as well as many single unattached men. Frankly, we don't know.

–*Leduc Representative*, February 18, 1947

The residents of the Leduc area, along with the rest of the population of Alberta, had every reason to be cautious and even a little skeptical about the possible riches of an oil strike. The Leduc strike of 1947 wasn't the first time someone had struck oil in Alberta and set off a torrent of speculation and excitement.

Dingman Well No. 1, owned by Calgary Petroleum Products Company, had struck oil on May 14, 1914, not too far from Turner Valley. Even though the wells were actually wet natural gas wells rather than typical oil wells (the gas was removed and the remaining oil could be easily used in automobiles with little refining), the discovery exploded into a Klondike-style boom that brought speculators of all types out of

Opening day of Imperial Leduc No. 1 discovery well, February 13, 1947

the woodwork. In one 24-hour period, more than 500 oil companies had been incorporated in Alberta by investors, promoters and hustlers looking to make a quick buck.

Although the initial news of the Turner Valley discovery was also subdued in the local newspapers—the *Okotoks Review* ran only a three-inch-long story on the back page of its May 15 edition—the quiet response to the oil strike didn't last.

Throughout the area, newspapers like the *Nanton News*, the *High River Times* and others had a plethora of articles on the strike. They discussed what it would mean to their area, the formation of oil companies by local businessmen and the possibility of drilling occurring near their towns.

The May 22, 1914, issue of the *Okotoks Review* featured a front page completely devoted to the discovery of oil and its implications. The three-line, all-caps banner headline read:

OKOTOKS THE CENTRE
OF THE OIL DISTRICTS
OF SOUTHERN ALBERTA

The proclamations of success and major growth in the town of Okotoks were no less bold, surpassing the typical boosterism of the average weekly of the time.

> *It is safe to say that there is no town in all the world today that offers the opportunities for investment that Okotoks does. The surrounding country is settled with a prosperous mixed farming population. That fact has kept Okotoks from being effected...by the recession that has damaged many other towns in the last two years.*

> *There are those who say, and that with good reason too, that Okotoks will rival Calgary as the City of the West and because nature has placed in such a favourable location she is destined to become the Oil Queen of North America. Situated right in the centre of the Oil Regions and in the hollow of the great territory that is tapped with oil wells. It is possible for oil to be taken from all the wells right in the town by natural gravitation. The great oil refineries will be built right here in Okotoks. Doubtless many other towns will make a bid to get part of the great development which this will mean, but Okotoks holds in her hand the mighty throttle of industry.*

> *–Okotoks Review*, May 22, 1914

Furthermore, the *Okotoks Review* changed its masthead to read *Okotoks Review and the Oilfields Record*.

At the same time, there were also a few voices of prudence and forethought. Since so many fledgling oil companies were swarming around, imploring local residents to invest and reap great rewards, the *High River Times*, which reported that the discovery could be a means for possible growth in the area, realized that several disreputable people were looking to make a quick buck on unsuspecting area residents. So the *Times* offered an editorial with advice on how to read a prospectus.

> *The intense excitement in connection with the recent find of oil in the province will now be the means of making many men rich and many more poor, and although in such times it is a difficult matter to get the general public to listen to reason, we feel it our duty nevertheless, to point out to the investor the salient points to be considered in reading a prospectus.*
>
> *We have no intention to "knock" any legitimate company, and we will even venture to say that investment in oil shares at the present seems to us to be a good investment, but there are grave dangers to be guarded against and we would like to explain as briefly as possible the chief points to be looked for in a prospectus.*
>
> *First is the treasury fund which is the amount to be devoted to development. These shares should be a reasonable proposition of the total capitalizations, say one-third.*
>
> *Second are the shares allotted to the vendors, which should not be put on the market until the treasury shares are sold.*
>
> *Third, to see that directors are capable and trustworthy men who can be relied upon.*
>
> *And lastly, the location of the property, for if this is not in a favorable position, the company is bound to go to the wall.*
>
> *All these points are equally important, and every investor should look carefully into these matters before putting his*

money into any company. We have seen several prospectuses that are so loosely drawn that the investor is hardly protected at all, and the only recommendation is that the directors are all thoroughly reliable and good business men, but greater care should be exercised in the drawing of prospectuses and we would warn all intending investors to be very careful as regards these points.

–High River Times, June 4, 1914

Although other wells were successfully drilled in the upcoming years and the Turner Valley oil field was, at the time, considered one of the largest in the British Empire, by February 22, 1917, the *Okotoks Review* dropped the *"Oilfields Record"* moniker in its name and went back to being simply the *Okotoks Review*. The promise of the Turner Valley oil fields did not translate into the riches that some people expected. World War I and the Great Depression played something of a role in that, preventing investment into more exploration and derailing plans to build a pipeline to eastern Canada, even though another successful oil discovery occurred in 1924. Oil prices did soar as a result of World War II, helping expand the Turner Valley Field in 1942, but by 1948, the area was pretty much tapped out.

In all, Turner Valley's total oil output totalled only 19 million cubic metres (just over 110 million barrels of oil). In comparison, the field beneath Leduc No. 1 produced over 50 million cubic metres (more than 300 million barrels of oil). And this time, the promised riches did come. Even larger oil and natural gas fields were discovered in other parts of the province.

The opening up of roads in previously remote areas of Alberta made petroleum finds in those parts of the province more economical. And the discovery of heavy oil in the tar sands in the northeastern areas of Alberta and the development of a means to extract that oil meant further prosperity, even as oil supplies were dwindling throughout the world.

The province transformed itself from a mostly agricultural economy to one of the major oil players of the 20th and 21st centuries.

Alberta, previously one of the perennial have-not provinces in Canada, became one of the drivers, not only of the Canadian economy but also its political system. And all of those events could be traced back to that February 6, 1947, rumour-based story in the *Leduc Representative*, the story that concerned an oil strike a few miles north of town.

～

YOUR REGIONAL COMMUNITY NEWSPAPER

℡ ✦CAPITAL

PUBLISHED IN THREE HILLS SINCE 1916

We acknowledge the financial support of the Government of Canada
through the Canada Periodical Fund (CPF) for our publishing activities.
Return undeliverable items to Capital Printers Ltd., Box 158, Three Hills, AB T0M 2A0

Canadä

CPF No. 40014706

The *Three Hills Capital* first hit the streets in 1916.

Hubert Peters was publisher/editor in those early days. An average weekly consisted of four to six pages, most of which a national news service provided in the form of pre-engraved lead plates. The front page was often the only page that contained any local news.

In 1922, C.H. Leathley took the helm. John A. Srathchan and Ed Rouleau followed in the 1930s, Claude J. Davidson in the 1940s and Barney Neutzling from about 1945 to 1956.

On February 8, 1956, R.V. (Bob) Dau and Wilfred J. (Porky) Schmidt purchased *The Capital*. The Dau family soon bought Schmidt's shares in the business.

Bob Dau remained as publisher/editor until his untimely passing in February 1977. His wife, Betty, carried on with the newspaper until Timothy Shearlaw was appointed as publisher in January 1980. Timothy and his wife Theresa purchased the company from the Dau family in May 1988 and have continued publishing to present day.

Being one of the oldest established businesses in Three Hills, one has to dig deep to uncover the paper's beginnings.

Up until the mid-1940s, *The Capital* was published from the building located directly behind the Royal Bank. It then moved to 523 Main Street where it remained for about 60 years.

In the early days, *The Capital* was printed in-house. Bob and Betty Dau purchased shares in a Calgary-based printing company called Perry Graphics. This was a great move for *The Capital* as it would now be printed on a large web press allowing 40 pages to be printed at one time. As the newspaper grew, this would prove very beneficial.

In the mid-1970s, Capital Printers Ltd. focused only on

newspaper work. At that time, a newspaper company was said to be worth more without a job plant than with one. In the 1980s and '90s, *The Capital* was printed at Central Alberta Publishers located at the Red Deer Industrial Airport.

The Capital is a regional community newspaper serving over 4500 subscribers each week. A contract was signed in April 1958 to supply a newspaper to all Municipal District of Kneehill #48 ratepayers (now known as Kneehill County). The contract was renewed each year and is now re-negotiated every three years. That boosted the paid circulation to 2300 upon the initial signing.

Following the purchase by the Shearlaws, distribution contracts were negotiated with the Town of Trochu, the Village of Linden, Village of Acme and most recently, the Village of Carbon. The Hamlets of Swalwell, Torrington, Wimborne and Huxley fall under the Kneehill County contract. The paper is read by a potential weekly audience of 11,000.

The Capital, at one time, used a promotional slogan, "What's Black and White and Read all Over?" But that changed in May 2002 when the printing was moved to Wainwright's *Star Press*. For the first time in the newspaper's history, colour pictures and display ads graced its pages. But this didn't come easily. Over the years, technology has played a major role in the success or failure of many community newspapers. From lead type and engraved pictures to digital computer imagery, the community newspaper has gone the distance.

In less than three decades, Tim Shearlaw has witnessed four eras in publishing. As a youngster he would perch outside the basement windows of Capital Printers Ltd. and watch as the paper was printed. The Linotype used in those days was demolished and removed, piece-by-piece, when Tim got his start in 1976.

The Capital was using paper tape Compuwriters that shook the building as column after column of type was produced. Production staff had to wear headphones because of the noise.

All the film and black-and-white photos were processed

in the paper's own darkroom. Advertising was produced with clip-art books and everything was "cut and paste." Glue sticks gave way as hot wax made its debut. Once the pages were laid out, negatives had to be processed before they could be rushed to the Calgary press operation.

Computerization made its first appearance at *The Capital* with the coming of Compugraphic typesetting equipment. These machines, called "Blue Boxes," revolutionized the newspaper business. Photosensitive paper was loaded into the machines, and type was transferred to the paper using a keyboard-activated strobe light and interchangeable font strips. One machine was used for news copy, one for classified and display ads and one for headlines.

In 1997, Capital Printers Ltd. installed its first two Mac computers, scanning system and laser printer. Gradually, production made the transition from total paste-up to digital.

The Shearlaws' eldest son, Jay, entered the business in 2000 and led the way in the transition to computerization. In May 2002, *The Capital* became totally electronic, including photography.

Now in its 96th year, *The Capital* moved to its new home at 411 Main Street on May 5, 2004. The last issue of the paper published at 523 Main Street was on Wednesday, April 28, 2004. In addition to publishing, *The Capital* also publishes several special issues such as Fire Prevention, Kneehill Grad Guide, and Salute to Agriculture.

Capital Printers Ltd., publishers of *The Capital*, is staffed by Timothy J. Shearlaw (1976), Theresa Shearlaw (1980), Barb Widmer (1985) and Jay Shearlaw (2000). Freelance reporter/photographer David Nadeau has been with the paper since September 1989. Reporter/photographer Debi Moon has been with the company since 1996. Grant Alford joined the staff as reporter/photographer in September 2011, as did Melinda Stevens.

If Tim has learned anything in the newspaper business. it's this: "If you think you've heard or seen everything, just wait until tomorrow." It's comparable to our Alberta weather.

CHAPTER FIFTEEN

The New Alberta

O IL WAS ONLY ONE FACTOR PROMPTING change in post-war Alberta. The residual effects of World War II were also beginning to be felt in the 1950s and early '60s. Although the war affected many Albertans personally, its impact was more deeply felt after the war ended. The character of Alberta's social, political and economic landscape was changing.

Although oil replaced agriculture as Alberta's economic driver, farmers in the province still made great strides. A rise in livestock, feed and produce prices convinced wheat farmers to diversify. The lack of manpower during the war forced farmers to rely on machinery, which in turn shifted Alberta's agriculture from mostly small, labour-intensive operations to larger operations requiring more mechanization and fewer workers.

Innovations such as the now ubiquitous combine turned a three-step process that involved eight to ten men into a one-step process with one operator and a couple of truck drivers, which was key in helping Alberta farmers adjust to the changing times.

Electricity also spread throughout the rural areas of the province, which had become somewhat of a hot issue in the late 1940s. Farmers wanted to install time-saving devices such as automatic systems for feeding, watering and milking their livestock as well as use appliances, radios,

Ernest Manning, premier of Alberta from 1943 to 1968

televisions and so on in their homes. With the cities and towns all powered up, most farmers wanted the same convenience. But the big question was who would pay to wire the countryside—the private power companies or the government?

To solve that issue, Premier Ernest Manning put the question to the electorate in the form of a plebiscite. Although the ruling Social Credit once again gained a huge majority in the election, Albertans in favour of private companies handling the electrification outnumbered those in favour of government control, by a mere 151 votes. Oddly enough, the vote was not split into a rural-urban issue but rather a north-south one. Around Calgary and the south, the vote favoured private ownership while in Edmonton and in the north, public ownership was preferred.

In the matter of rural electrification it will be interesting to see how the government interprets the plebiscite. It was not an overwhelming expression of public opinion. We'll settle for some system similar to the rural telephone operation in Alberta now. We doubt if the Government will take on the purchase of existing generating plants.

–*Camrose Canadian*, August 18, 1948

One of the things that is getting as little publicity as possible in the forth-coming election is the referendum on the part of the government to take over the distribution of electrical power in the province. The C.C.F. [Co-operative Commonwealth Federation] claim that this is a plank in their platform that the government have stolen. Be that as it may, the plank is not too strong.

Here in Olds we are getting pretty cheap power from the Calgary Power Co. Well most of us are satisfied, but the thing is to consider is whether or not we would have as cheap a power and as good a service after the government had gone out and borrowed money to buy the Calgary Power layout. With interests going up on borrowing money, we hardly think that this would be possible. Right now we are probably handling the shareholders of Power Co. stock a goodly return on their investment every month. But buy these investor out with more borrowed money and over a period of twenty or thirty years and see how much you would be paying to the investors. Yes investors, for who else can buy the bonds that the government would be required to sell to buy the Power Co. out. Certainly not you and me, but we would pay for it in the end.

Oh yes, and if the government were to form small power Co-ops to operate the lines, we wonder how successful they would be. Haven't the people had enough grief handling the telephone lines handed to them by a patronizing government?

Mary Readman and daughter Carol Bruha at 75th AWNA annual convention in 1995

Vote Social Credit if that is the way you want. Vote C.C.F. if you desire. Or vote liberal, or Independent or Labor progressive, but don't be taken in on the power plebiscite. There are many other things we need before we need the power companies in the hands of we the people. For one thing we need more market roads such as we have in this constituency, we need a greater amount of industry in the province to make use of our natural resource, we need above else a first class road from north to south and from east the west, one that won't be torn up every summer to be repaired. With the expansion of the oil industry in this province, it is about time we had these roads.

–*Olds Gazette*, August 5, 1948

Although electricity was a hot topic, nothing was hotter than roads. Vehicle ownership skyrocketed after World War II, with annual new car sales in Alberta rising from 11,000 in 1948 to over 40,000 in 1958.

Highways and roads in the 1940s and '50s, however, were in terrible shape with barely 1045 kilometres of paved roads throughout the province. To get anywhere in Alberta, especially in rural areas, drivers had to use gravel roads that washed out in the summer rains and were covered in snow the entire winter. Even the main highway between Calgary and Edmonton, the two-lane Highway 2 (now called Highway 2A), could be impassable at times. Although paved, Highway 2 suffered break-ups during the spring thaw and had to undergo major repairs during most of the summers. Winter driving could also be treacherous.

So in the post-war period, Albertans wanted new roads and all the upgrades that came with them, such as overpasses, better signage, new bridges and so on.

A letter published elsewhere on this page states that the ferry at Dunvegan is "one of the finest available in its class" and continued that "it could give reasonable good service if it had the proper ferry operators."

Now as the editor of the Post, *I am not backing down from the fact that I believe a bridge should be built at Dunvegan, because of regardless of how good a ferry may be, it can never take the place of a bridge. However if all the facts in the letter are true and I have no reason to doubt them, then something should be done to see that, until a bridge is built, the ferry service is brought to high standard as possible.*

Just a week ago the ferry broke loose from the tug when a cable snapped, with the result that two cars bringing home a girls' softball team from a sports day, drifted helplessly down the river for approximately one hour before the tug was able to bring the ferry back under control.

Some of girls on the ferry were given a very bad scare which is understandable when you consider that only a few weeks ago two women were drowned in a ferry accident at Watino recently.

This type of thing is deplorable. All cables, fittings, lifeboats and mechanical parts of the ferry should be checked daily. There is absolutely no excuse for mishaps of this nature.

Accidents of this type cost lives and if they occur because of laxity on the parts of servants of the Alberta department of highways, then the time has come for us to demand action.

Now that the election date has been set for August 5, I repeat my claim that all persons interested in a bridge at Dunvegan should make it a point to get a definite statement from the various candidates seeking election or re-election as to whether or not it is their intention to do everything within their power to get a bridge at Dunvegan if elected to office.

–Fairview Post, July 10, 1952

With oil revenues coming in, and in reaction to increased use of automobiles, the Alberta government responded. Spending on highway construction increased to almost $50 million per year. Although many arterial highways and secondary highways were paved or upgraded during this boom period (including the construction of the Dunvegan Bridge in 1960), probably the biggest road construction development in Alberta was the new road built between Edmonton and Calgary. The province also played a role in the development of the Trans-Canada Highway, but the new four-lane "interstate"-style highway (later called Highway 2 and now named the Queen Elizabeth II Highway) between Alberta's two major cities, Edmonton and Calgary, would eclipse that.

In order to ensure a quick trip for motorists, the province's plan called for the highway to bypass many of the small towns that presently sat near or along the old Highway 2, which is now known as Highway 2A.

Reaction to the new highway was mixed. Albertans, even those in towns being bypassed, liked the idea of a quick route between Edmonton and Calgary. But they also worried about the impact it would have on business.

> *Driving home from the south the other morning we were more than impressed by the fine four-lane highway and the very attractive and conspicuous green and white signs that give motorists a guide to the towns that are not on the main stem. 'Twas easy enough to figure where to turn off if we had to visit either Airdrie, Crossfield, Beiseker or Carstairs. But there the holiday ended as far as we were concerned. Driving towards "our town" we had to use our bifocals to read the wee sign pointing towards "our town." The government has provided us with a fine hardtop trail leading our way; would it be too much to ask that they now produce one of those attractive directional signs so travelers can make use of the new road and visit with us.*
>
> *–Didsbury Pioneer,* October 30, 1958

Farther north, the situation with the new highway rankled the town of Wetaskiwin. With the southern leg of the new road completed in 1958, planning now turned to the northern section. Although Wetaskiwin was concerned about the increased traffic a new highway would bring through their town, residents hoped it would be built close enough so that motorists wouldn't have to travel a major distance to stop in town.

> *Our way of life has always centred around transportation and any community that expects to grow and expand must be reasonably close to the main transportation routes.*
>
> *Wetaskiwin did not just "happen" to be here. It was first only a siding of the railway being built between Calgary and Edmonton. Without the railroad, that era's most important method of transportation, Wetaskiwin would never have been born. Nor would it have grown to be such an important centre in this part of the province.*

It is just as important today that this community be close to main transportation routes as it was then. There is no doubt that highways are replacing the railways for the movement of people and produce from one place to another and a community that is not reasonably close to a main highway route will have found a remarkable cure for its growing pains.

If we believe that a part of the community can suffer without the whole being affected we are only kidding ourselves. The loss of highway business will leave a gaping hole in our community that will have repercussions for all city businesses and every dollar that does not reach this important section of our economy on the highway will be multiplied many times over.

If highways are to be useful they should serve ALL the people and particularly the main centres of the area through which they pass.

Wetaskiwin should never expect any lesser service from any government.

–Wetaskiwin Times, November 22, 1961

The initial plan of building the highway almost nine kilometres from Wetaskiwin didn't sit well with the community, but when the final decision was made, the new highway would be 16 kilometres from Wetaskiwin. Many communities that had served the old highway were now bypassed. Residents in the area saw it as a sign that the government was more interested in developing the major cities of the province and that rural areas were second place in terms of economic expansion.

From a population point of view, that urban-rural change had already occurred. The post-war boom not only brought prosperity to the province, but it also attracted more people and a change in the demographic. Although Alberta's population didn't increase substantially during the war years, by 1951 more than half of the province's citizens lived in urban areas. Edmonton and Calgary kept growing as new subdivisions sprang up

From left to right: Bill Draayer (*Wetaskiwin Times*), former prime minister L.B. Pearson and Roy Willis (*Stettler Independent*), Banff, 1959

on what used to be farmland. Other cities such as Lethbridge, Medicine Hat and Red Deer also expanded. Many towns, such as Camrose, grew from a pre-war population of 2600 to more than 7000 by 1961.

Despite the economic growth of the province, the future of the newspaper business seemed extremely unsure. The proliferation of television as an advertising medium was thought to be the death knell for traditional media. Radio suffered greatly because of television, and it was thought that newspapers would not last in the new media age to come.

On January 20, 1951, Alberta's first newspaper, the *Edmonton Bulletin*, published its final issue. Its founder, Frank Oliver, died in 1933, but he had sold out his shares in the *Bulletin* 10 years earlier. At the time of the paper's demise, Calgarian Max Bell owned the daily *Bulletin* as well

Printing office of the *Crossfield Chronicle*, ca. 1912

as the *Calgary Albertan*. Circulation had increased at the *Bulletin* during Bell's tenure but advertising revenues did not. The *Bulletin*'s main competitor, the *Edmonton Journal*, was part of the more business-oriented Southam chain and had access to more lucrative national advertising. And Edmonton, like many other Canadian cities at the time, could only support one paper, so the *Bulletin* was shut down.

Some people in the media industry felt that small-town weekly newspapers would go the way of other papers like the *Bulletin*.

But a major shift was occurring in the community weekly throughout Alberta. A new generation of publishers, editors and reporters, mostly young men in their 20s and 30s, were taking over from the earlier generation who had been operating and working for their respective newspapers since the 1920s and '30s. Many of these newspapermen were veterans of World War II, and after they came back home, they weren't content with continuing the family business or farm. They were looking for careers that provided more meaning and interest to their lives. A good number of them looked to the newspaper industry.

A few of the veterans, such as John Gordon, Bert Ford, Ronnie Newsom and others, had previously worked in the newspaper industry and returned to careers in Alberta weeklies. Bert Ford ran the *Lacombe Globe* until his death in 1974. Like his father Leonard Newsom, Ronnie worked at a variety of newspapers, first as a partner with Neil Leatherdale in the *Olds Gazette* and the *Crossfield Chronicle*, until 1957 when he bought the *Bashaw Star*. Newsom remained at the *Star* until 1973, leaving not long after the death of his first wife, Myrtle. Newsom moved to Calgary and became the editor of the *Strathmore Bow Valley Standard* at Heritage Park until 1984. He passed away in 2004 at the age of 90.

Some, like Neil Leatherdale, Ken Patrige (*Camrose Canadian*), Doug Caston (*Edson Leader, Hinton Herald*) and John Snuggs (*South Side Mirror*), to name a few, came to Alberta because of the war. Many of them served in some capacity in the RAF and the RCAF, which had several flight training facilities in the province, and when the war ended, they either remained in Alberta or came back after being demobilized.

Other men, some originally from Alberta and some not, had spent time overseas and were open to new opportunities and ideas that were not present before the war. Some were too young to have served but old enough to feel the effects of a global war and realized they didn't have to accept how things were done in the old days—a new world of possibilities lay ahead of them. And for some of these people, owning or managing a weekly newspaper in the wide open lands of western rural Canada seemed like the perfect option, even if it was only for a short period of time.

This diverse group of people, this next generation of Alberta weekly newspaper owners, publishers, editors, printers and reporters, strengthened and continued to build the Alberta weekly newspaper industry.

Jellis Block, Edson, 1911. The first *Edson Leader* newspaper was printed here. (Office of Edson Lumber Company on right; manager Bill York in doorway)

They proved wrong the naysayers who predicted the demise of the weekly newspaper during the advent of newer technology and faster communication.

Even with the introduction of television and improved communications, the weekly newspaper was still a vital part of Alberta communities. The problem with the prediction of the death of weeklies was that the doomsayers didn't truly understand the role of the weekly newspaper in a small town.

CHAPTER SIXTEEN

A Place in the Community

IN THE SPRING OF 1960, THE CANADIAN Weekly Newspapers Association (CWNA) conducted a study on the readership of the average Canadian weekly. For this study, the *Lacombe Globe* was chosen. Founded by Charles "Barney" Halpin in 1903, the paper was known originally as the *Lacombe Western Globe*. Halpin owned the newspaper until 1935 when he sold it to Harry J. Ford, who served as president of the Alberta chapter of the CWNA for 1939–40. After Harry's death in 1948, his sons Bert and Tom took over operations of the *Globe*. Following in his father's footsteps, Bert was elected president of the Alberta chapter for 1952–53.

At the time, the 1960 readership survey was a landmark study. The CWNA had conducted a smaller study in 1956, but it dealt with the readership of the *Bowmanville Canadian Statesman*, a predominantly urban weekly based 75 kilometres east of Toronto. Before the Lacombe study, never before had the readership of a rural Canadian weekly been thoroughly analyzed.

The *Lacombe Globe* was chosen because it was, according to the study's author, Dr. Gordon Hirabayashi, head of the Sociology Department at the University of Alberta, "a paper with circulation that is neither atypically large or small in relation to other Canadian weekly newspapers. A paper serving a trading area divorced from major metropolitan centres which might introduce atypical factors."

In March 1960, more than 80 sociology and psychology students from the University of Alberta did most of the fieldwork, interviewing many of the 2400-plus subscribers of the *Lacombe Globe* at that time.

What the study found may have surprised advertisers, but not the newspaper publishers. It was determined that more than 95 percent of the households in Lacombe subscribed to the *Globe*. Additionally, almost one-third of those subscribers passed the paper to someone else who lived in another household. Furthermore, the majority of the readership also noted that they read every single inch of the newspaper, which included all the articles and display ads plus every classified ad.

And finally, and more importantly, at least from an advertising point of view, almost 90 percent of the readers in the study said they accepted the credibility of the information in the newspaper, including claims made in the advertisements.

The study was a resounding support of the weekly newspapers as a highly credible advertising medium; however, the study did not answer the question of why Lacombe residents read their local paper with such voracity. And for some academics and historians, this was puzzling.

"One might surmise, that the rural weekly fulfilled its mission by providing news of a purely local nature," wrote University of Alberta professor Paul Voisey in his book, *High River and the Times*.

> *But such a presumption would be mistaken, for although the weekly presented a plethora of local items by providing news of a purely local nature, they were rarely "news" to its readers. In rural communities where "everyone knows everyone," word of mouth effectively relayed recent events, especially after telephone lines invaded the countryside. Most people already knew about the big fire, the grisly accident or the birth of twins*

before reading about it in the local weekly. Even the hermit,
who went nowhere and spoke to no one, learned nothing from
reading that "a heavy snowfall blanketed the district last Sat-
urday" or that "crops are looking good this year."

Voisey later added, "Now the mystery deepens: readers avidly devoured newspapers that served no apparent purpose.... The rural press apparently satisfied psychological and social longings that other forms of media did not."

But, as noted, the results of the study did not surprise the weekly newspaper publishers at that time, and neither would they be surprised today. The results of the study confirmed the claims that they had been making for years, especially that the subscribed circulation of a weekly did not reflect how many people read the paper because each issue is normally passed on several times within a household and then given to other households that are not subscribers.

Why residents read the local weekly, or what the role of the paper was in the community, are not questions that publishers/editors worry about too much because they know their community. They know the people, almost everyone by name, as well as the groups and organizations that ensure the town functions. The readers are often part of these organizations and/or have spearheaded many local developments. And with this knowledge and connection, weekly newspapers publish a paper that isn't just something for residents to read, it is an integral part of the community.

"People who read weeklies are looking for facts. Weeklies do not need the sensational; they carry the news the people want to read," said Ken Patrige, co-owner of the *Camrose Canadian* in 1964. "The weekly publisher, and I am thinking of those who are doing the job as it should be done, is in a position to paint an accurate word picture of what is happening in his community. He knows the people, he knows their habits and knows the facts behind what he considers news."

You hardly let out your first yell on this terrestrial sphere before the local editor ordered the fact of your arrival announced to a baby-loving world.

When you reached the age of three or four and had your first real birthday party with invited guests, your friend, the editor, told all and sundry who was there and what a fuss they made over you.

When you got on the honour roll at grade school he let all your admiring neighbours know about it. If you got into any minor scrapes he apparently forgot about them as soon as he was told, for he wanted to play up the things which might make you great.

All through your high-school course he was keenly watching to see if you did anything worthy of note in athletics, letters or debate. And when you finally graduated, he again seized upon the opportunity to put your name in print.

If you decided to go to work then, instead of going to college, he heralded the fact in such a manner that made any prospective employers realize that here was an ambitious lad who wasn't leaning unnecessarily on the folks. He wanted all of whom it might concern to know that if work was to be done, here was a live-wire all set.

When the supreme object of your heart's desire was won your editor friend seemed to know about it almost as soon as the "lucky" girl and warned all other aspirants to her attention to lay off as he printed the announcement of your engagement. Once more you were the conquering hero or thought so. The girl may have had other ideas on the subject.

If after you accomplished anything worthy of note, the world was told in letters bold: "Home Town Boy Makes Good."

From left to right: Ken Patrige (*Camrose Canadian*), Fred Johns (*Leduc Representative*), Chuck MacLean (*Camrose Canadian*), Bob Munro (*Hanna Herald*), Bert Ford (*Lacombe Globe*) and Ben Knowles, CWNA Convention, Lethbridge, 1950

When those near and dear to you were, by death, taken out on "The Great Adventure," the Chief of Columns apparently forgot about their vices and proceeded to laud their virtues and remind the world of their fine family connections— including you.

When illness overtook you, he let all the neighbours know, so that may-haps the power of their prayers could be added to the forces of medicine.

And someday (should he perchance outlive you as he has so many others) he, being kind and faithful unto the end, will once more probably tell mankind far and wide that one has passed who was a faithful and worthwhile addition to the race, that you have gone to join the glorious company who become the "guests of God."

Yes, from cradle of birth to the casket of death, the home town editor is your friend. He puts you on the map, and if you are worthy, helps to keep you there.

–Blairmore Enterprise, July 18, 1935

School for Journalists

Ron Newsom, the long-time publisher of the *Bashaw Star*, was not only one of the major contributors to the continued strengthening and promotion of weekly newspapers in the province, but he was also behind one development that had a lasting impact on the sustainment of the industry: the first Alberta school for journalists.

"Organizing this first school of journalism was a joint project of SAIT (Southern Alberta Institute of Technology) and the Alberta Weekly Newspapers Association. It was the brainchild of the then-president of the association, Ron Newsom," wrote veteran newspaper publisher George Meyer in his book, *A Prairie Publisher: My 56 Years of Printing and Publishing in Alberta.* "Ron spent a lot of time organizing the creation of the SAIT School of Journalism. The project, as far as the AWNA was concerned, was a way to mark the 60th anniversary of the province of Alberta in 1965. I am sure that Ron had been working on it long before he became president of the AWNA in the fall of 1964."

Prior to the development of the journalism program at the SAIT, Alberta weeklies hired editors and reporters from a wide variety of sources and locales. Some were university grads with a degree in English looking to a rural weekly as a stepping-stone into the world of daily journalism. Many wouldn't last long. Another good source for editors and reporters were the contributors that the average weekly relied on to provide news about the outlying areas it covered. If one of these contributors proved to have more talent or ambition than average, an editor or publisher would "promote" them to a reporter position and pay them a small wage. Newspapers also often looked to their own family members—sons, daughters or grandchildren—who showed aptitude or interest in the newspaper business.

Community papers also relied on other newspaper families to recruit editors and reporters who had been raised in the business and were looking to strike out on their own. And there are plenty

Ron Newsom (*Bashaw Star*) and wife Louise at the AWNA's 75th anniversary, 1995

of stories about printers or their apprentices who made the move from the back shop to the front, George Meyer being one of them.

But despite these available options for finding editors and reporters, other reliable sources had to be found. If Alberta weeklies were going to move forward in the final half of the 20th century, they had to create a place that would develop such personnel.

So in 1964, an advisory committee from the AWNA was established, and Ralph Brinsmead, a former reporter at the *Camrose Canadian*, became the first director of the recruiting program in 1965. Many members of the advisory committee as well as other Alberta weekly publishers and editors were asked to lecture to the students about working at a small-town paper. From the beginning (and even up to current times), the SAIT program was designed specifically for graduates to gain employment at a rural weekly newspaper.

"One thing I remember stipulating for the school in the days when we were planning the curriculum was that it not be equipped with new typewriters and any other new equipment in the print shop," wrote Meyer in *A Prairie Publisher.* "The thinking behind this suggestion was that the students would learn to run old equipment, because that is all they would see in their first jobs, if those jobs happened to be in a weekly or a daily newspaper. I had the backing of every newspaper publisher on the committee on that one. More than 30 years later, the SAIT Journalism Arts program has graduated thousands of students, many of whom went on to work at weekly newspapers in Alberta and around the country."

Frank McTighe was one of those students; he enrolled in the SAIT Journalism Arts program in 1978. "[SAIT] got me well prepared to go out to a small paper. I felt that even after our first year, they had given us our skills to go out and work in a community newspaper," he says.

After SAIT and a brief stint in the composing room of the *Calgary Herald,* McTighe worked at a variety of southern Alberta newspapers, including the *Taber Times, High River Times, Nanton News* and *Vauxhall Advance.* And in 1995, McTighe returned to SAIT, this time as a news-writing instructor. He spent five years in that position before purchasing the *Macleod Gazette,* where he is the current publisher.

CHAPTER SEVENTEEN

A New Era

WHEN THE 1960S ENDED AND ALBERTA headed into the last few decades of the 20th century, the rumblings of political change were in the air. After more than 35 years of rule by the Social Credit, Albertans were looking for a more modern type of politician and political will to reflect the progressive attitude that was advancing throughout the province.

Calgary lawyer Peter Lougheed was the grandson of Sir James Alexander Lougheed, a member of the federal Conservative Party who had campaigned for Sir John A. Macdonald. For many years, Sir James Lougheed served in the Senate, gaining the respect of his fellow colleagues for his strong and unwavering support of the Canadian West. Peter inherited his grandfather's strong values. But before he could stand in support of the West and Alberta, the province of his birth, young Peter Lougheed had to gain political power. During his rise as a politician, it wasn't a good time to be a member of the Conservative Party in Alberta.

In the 1963 election, not a single Conservative had won a seat. Prior to that, the party had only one member in the Legislature. But Lougheed was a new kind of politician—young and urbane with a law degree from the University of Alberta and a MBA from Harvard. He not only had

Peter Lougheed, premier of Alberta from 1971 to 1985

a family history for name recognition, but he had also been a member of the Edmonton Eskimos in the 1950s and was known for his scrappy play despite being one of the smallest players in the Canadian Football League.

In 1965, Lougheed was named leader of the Progressive Conservative Party. In the 1967 election, the PCs went from having no seats in the legislature to having six and becoming the official opposition. That election also marked the last time Social Credit leader Ernest Manning would put his name on a ballot. In 1968, Manning resigned as leader, and Harry Strom took his place.

On the other side of the legislature, Lougheed expanded his base with a couple of by-election wins, and the 1971 election was becoming one of the closest fought since the middle of the Great Depression almost 40 years earlier. For the first time in years, no one was taking the chance to say which party would win the election. There was still the sense that Alberta wasn't completely ready for a dramatic change and that the Social Credit would remain in power, at least for the time being.

> *Some two months ago we predicted that an Alberta election would be held in August, at that time other media were forecasting a fall election date. Monday they began to put all the signs together and are now joining us in our prediction.*
>
> *During the months of July and August Albertans by the thousands are fanning out across Canada and the US and even in Europe and Asia. Most are returning with one dominating view—that Alberta is a pretty good place to live and there isn't much wrong with the present Provincial administration.*
>
> *Strong undercurrents of a "change for the sake of change" have given way to an even stronger tide that is quietly asking "will change be for the better?"*
>
> *Anyone who has or will visit Saskatchewan during the summer will find residents wondering what their change is going to bring them. They will tell you that the NDP victory at the polls was nothing more than a rejection of the personal qualities of the former Premier R. Thatcher. They tell you he was blunt, sarcastic, adamant and dictatorial. They agree with the policies he presented but not his methods. At the same time, they have their fingers crossed hoping that the NDP regime will continue policies enunciated and put into action by Thatcher's Liberals.*
>
> *Saskatchewan has shown that change carries with it the element of risk. However, elections give people the right and duty to accept or reject the old or the new.*

Alberta's 1971 election carries with it all the elements of political hope and despair. More importantly, the election will shape our destiny for the coming years.

–Olds Gazette, July 22, 1971

Given these sentiments, it was shocking when Peter Lougheed became premier of Alberta, winning 49 of the 75 seats up for grabs.

All good things must come to an end, or so the saying goes, And voters have ended a 36-year stay in power for the Social Credit Party in Alberta. It is surprising to find such a large number of Progressive Conservative voters in our area. It seems that everyone voted that way. But then it is fashionable to be on the winning side.

The upset by Peter Lougheed's P.C.'s poses some interesting questions. Some will take upwards to four years to answer while some will be resolved sooner.

For example: Can anyone guess as to what will happen to Provincial Treasury Branches. They are a Socred idea, and against the P.C. free enterprise system.

If and where will a Senior Citizen Lodge be built in this constituency? It was an underlying local election issue.

Can Harry Strom and his experienced M.L.A.s fill the roll of Opposition. Will our newly elected M.L.A. be as effective or will he perform better as a member of the opposition?

Will the Progressive Conservatives, who are novices at the game, be able to give good government? Will their stewardship till next election time be impressive enough to re-elect or will the Socreds go back in?

My predictions were all wrong, re August 30, but it'll be an interesting "wait and see."

–Sedgewick Community Press, September 9, 1971

The sudden rejection of the Social Credit Party by the province's electorate, will provide cause for much controversy during the coming months. It is a situation such as this which helps to make politics such an exciting forum.

The pundits will have a field day expressing their views as to the reason why the Social Credit movement was so dramatically cast aside after more than thirty-six years of conducting the affairs of Alberta.

We think the very fact the government had held office for so long a period is high on the list of items which led to its defeat. We are of the opinion we have seen the last of the days when one political party, whether provincial or federal, will be able to remain in continuous control for an extended period of time.

–Claresholm Local Press, September 2, 1971

Alberta saw unprecedented growth in the next decade and a half. The energy crisis that struck the Western world in the '70s created a surge in development throughout the province. Oil and gas exploration skyrocketed, with construction of new refineries and plants and expansion into more diverse products such as natural gas and sulphur refined from sour gas wells. The huge development of the tar sands in northeastern Alberta pressed forward as the province looked to become a major supplier of petroleum products during a time when other resources were either drying out or being controlled by embargos.

Money poured into the provincial coffers and the Lougheed government was not afraid to spend. Capital projects such as building roads, schools, hospitals, arenas and community centres proliferated across the province. Edmonton and Calgary grew from sleepy Western Canadian towns to major metropolitan areas complete with sprawling suburbs. Small town and rural residents also gained from the economic boom.

From left to right: Jack Gieg (*Leduc Representative*), Jack Parry (*Rimbey Record*), Al Willis (*Stettler Independent*) and Chuck MacLean (*Camrose Canadian*) at the 1981 AWNA convention

Many communities, which may have had local newspapers in the past, only to see them fold because the population and economic base was too small to sustain them, saw a resurgence in the popularity of community news. The period following the 1971 election to 1982 saw the founding of more than 80 community newspapers throughout the province.

These newer community newspapers, including the *Airdrie and District Echo*, *Bowden Eye Opener*, *Okotoks Western Wheel*, *Mayerthorpe Freelancer*, *Redwater Tribune* and *Viking Review*, are now considered solid examples of quality and award-winning journalism and long-time, contributing members of their respective communities.

Started by Ed and Wanda Cowley, the first edition of the *Mayerthorpe Freelancer* was distributed on April 4, 1978. The newspaper's office was first located in Greencourt, then Sangudo and was finally moved to a converted house in Mayerthorpe.

The Cowleys operated the newspaper for several years before selling the publication to Lynard Publishers of Leduc. After the sale, Ed and Wanda first moved to Stony Plain and eventually to Redwater.

Lynard Publishers, under the direction of Howie Bowes, purchased the operation in 1986. Jack Geig, Mr. Bowes' associate and long-time newspaperman, erected a new building for the newspaper at its present location. Geig owns the building to this day and directly oversaw the operations of the newspaper under the direction of general manager Ellen Wilson, who continued to handle sales duties.

Howie's brother Jim Bowes of Bowes Publishers Ltd. purchased Lynard Publishers in 1989. Since that time, Bowes Publishers Ltd. was acquired by Sun Media.

Front office manager Lorraine Dwyer joined the paper in 1986. Ellen Wilson continued as general manager until retiring in early 1992. Present publisher Jim Gray arrived in March 1992 from the *Fort McMurray Today*, where he was ad manager.

The *Freelancer*, as with most newspaper publications, has had its share of ups and downs. The BSE scare, along with a few years of drought, affected the publication, as agriculture in general and cow-calf operations in particular are the driving force of the local economy. However, the newspaper is now recovering from those lean years.

The most dramatic story over the years was, of course, the tragic loss of four RCMP officers at the hands of a crazed local gunman on March 3, 2005. The community and the newspaper are still recovering from that tragedy. Mayerthorpe is building a new future. The Mayerthorpe Fallen Four Memorial Society continues to raise funds for a memorial and park dedicated to the "Fallen Four."

The *Mayerthorpe Freelancer* is a paid circulation weekly, distributed on Wednesdays in Mayerthorpe, Blue Ridge, Anselmo, Rochfort Bridge, Sangudo, Cherhill and surrounding area, with advertising sales in those communities, plus Barrhead and Whitecourt.

The newspaper looks forward to continue serving the community as both continue to grow.

The Alberta Weekly Newspapers Association also took major steps during these growing economic times. "Before the mid-70s, the AWNA was very much an old boys' club," says current AWNA executive director Dennis Merrell in an interview for this book. "The guys would get together and have a few drinks and occasionally get together with the premier and his cabinet and argue why they should be buying more ads in their newspapers or whatever the issue of the day that weekly editors were concerned about, and thought the Province of Alberta should also be concerned."

A number of years earlier, the Manitoba Community Newspapers Association (MCNA) came up with a plan that allowed individuals and businesses to purchase a classified ad that would appear in every newspaper of the association. In short, you could place a classified ad of any type in one town, and for a few dollars more, "blanket" the entire province with the same ad. The newspaper that originally took the order for the ad received a finder's fee, but most of the profit from the ads went to the MCNA for the administration of the plan and other programs that the association offered or could develop. Unfortunately, the Manitoba blanket experiment failed because not enough member newspapers were interested in the idea.

However, the Alberta Weekly Newspapers Association still saw value in the plan and found a means to implement it. And they also found a way to ensure that member newspapers would support it. "After giving the proposal a chance to 'soak in,' there was a follow-up letter specifically asking members to sign up and become part of the program. Enclosed this time was a form calling upon the member to indicate his/her approval and to agree to the terms of payment," wrote George Meyer in his book *A Prairie Publisher*. "Well aware of the lack of response and/or procrastination of some of our members in the past, I stated that on the form what the deadline for a reply would be and that if there was no response by that deadline, 'it will be taken as the member's approval.'"

Bill Draayer (*Wetaskiwin Times*), in the late 1950s

The ploy worked, and the blanket classifieds program became one of the core programs of the AWNA. "It was the economic engine of the association because George convinced the publishers to run these classifieds so that the revenue would go to association activities and pay for the cost of running the affairs of the association," explains Dennis Merrell.

The blanket classifieds program became so successful that the volunteer executive of the AWNA had to hire someone to run the program and help develop other programs for the association using the monies raised through blanket classifieds.

Another person to take an active role in the AWNA was Bill Draayer. Born in Swift Current, Saskatchewan, on New Year's Eve in 1906, Draayer already had a long and successful history with Alberta newspapers. Following stints with the *Regina Leader-Post* and the *Regina Daily Star*, Draayer moved to Wetaskiwin in 1942 and bought the *Wetaskiwin Times*, which he published and edited for 25 years. He was also a key member of the Canadian Weekly Newspapers Association, first serving as a director and then as president, from 1956 to 1957.

In 1965, Draayer left the newspaper business for a while, selling the *Times* to Ken Patrige and Chuck MacLean, the long-time publishers of the *Camrose Canadian*. Draayer moved to Edmonton to work for the provincial government in the Department of Health, the Workers' Compensation Board and the Alcohol and Drug Abuse Commission. In 1976, he returned to his weekly newspaper roots and became the first secretary-manager of the AWNA.

For the first time, the AWNA had a central office in Edmonton, and Draayer was instrumental in introducing readership surveys, creating data books, requiring that all AWNA members have their circulation numbers audited and developing programs such as the One Order-One Bill system for national advertising agencies. "And that's when the association began acting as a broker and placing national advertising in member newspapers," notes Merrell. "And that's what caught the members' attention. They were receiving actual advertisements and more importantly, money, because of the association."

Draayer remained as secretary-manager of the AWNA until 1982, a year that had special meaning to Alberta weeklies because it was the centennial of the *Macleod Gazette*, a weekly founded by former North-West Mounted Police officers Charles E.D. Wood and E.T. "Si" Saunders. At the time, it was the longest-running newspaper in Alberta and still holds that title.

> *I guess it was bound to happen, although through the years there have been times when it looked like I would never even see the next issue, much less another volume.*

But here it is, Volume 100, and the opportune time for reflection and soul searching.

I wish C.E.D. [Charles E.D. Wood] could be here. I don't suppose he ever envisioned the Gazette reaching the milestone it has today, as he laboured over putting out Vol. 1, No. 1 back on July 1, 1882.

Things were different then, back on the original fort site when the town of Fort Macleod was in its 8th year of existence and the paper was in its infancy. The arduous task of handsetting all the type for each issue, letter by letter, was a far cry from the revolutionary line casting machines, more commonly known as the linotypes, that appeared in the early 1900's. Now, even the linotype has gone the way of the dinosaur.

The rigors of pioneer printing were such that many typesetters were known to imbibe and were frowned upon in that day's society. They often became tramp printers, moving from shop to shop until boredom overcame them once again. Today, there are fewer late nights and the modern typesetters are usually working women with husbands and kids and a home to clean up after a day in the shop. A holdover from the old days would be the cold beer a beleaguered editor seeks following the successful meeting of yet another deadline.

And, as for the actual printing of the paper well...old C.E.D. would recall the days when we'd hire several darker-skinned Peigan lads to turn the big press over hand by hand and print the Gazette. Boy did we make them work. But not today, pasting up news strips and ads on ruled out page sheets and shooting this product on a large camera to produce a negative which then is converted to a plate for clamping in place on a huge newspaper press capable of running off the entire Gazette in 20 minutes is a far cry from the old hot metal procedure.

Yes there have been many high points and low points in my century of being, but it's all been worth it. I've been read by royalty and some of the tops heads of government but I still get my greatest satisfaction from little children rusting through the paper to show their parents the picture of their school class or such like. Odds are, that at my age, their grandparents had done the same thing when they were tots.

But, I'm a little tired now, this crew that takes credit for my publication these days has been crawling all over my old bones for 18 to 20 hours a day for the past few weeks trying to get this special edition out and I've just about had it.

Besides, I need to rest. I'm about to start work on my second century.

–Macleod Gazette, July 1, 1982

Peter Lougheed finished his tenure as premier three years later in 1985, ending an era of growth and prosperity for the province. The *Claresholm Local Press* got it wrong in their statement that Alberta had seen the last of the days when one party would stay in power for too long. Although the PCs were considered a new party when it took over from the Social Credit in 1971, the concept of one-party rule continued in Alberta.

After Lougheed came Don Getty, followed by Ralph Klein and Ed Stelmach, different leaders of the same party. The PC Party banner has ruled Alberta even longer than the Social Credit, marking their 40th year in power in 2011 and still counting.

For the final 15 or so years of the 20th century and into Alberta's centennial in 2005, the province had a breather from experiencing major historical changes and events. The economy dipped and rose, deficits grew and were slain, but in the grand scheme of Alberta's 100 years, when compared to the two world wars, the Spanish influenza, the Depression and the political battles that changed the province, Alberta lived through times of relative calm.

And it was during this time of historical quiet in the province that the weekly newspaper industry faced a whole new set of challenges. The end of the Lougheed era in Alberta politics in 1985 marked a transitional period in Alberta weeklies, one that not only revolutionized the industry but also rocked it to its core.

~

CHAPTER EIGHTEEN

Turn and Face the Change

T HE ALBERTA WEEKLY NEWSPAPERS ASSOCIATION went through significant changes in the early 1980s, and over the next couple of decades it went through many more.

First, the association's original executive director, Bill Draayer, retired in 1982 and was replaced by Dennis Merrell, who still retains the position. Originally from Manitoba, Merrell studied business administration in university and then journalism at a community college. For a couple of years he worked as a reporter/photographer at a Manitoba weekly, so he was familiar with the operation of a Canadian community weekly. He also spent several years as an account executive at Edmonton's largest advertising agency and saw things from the unique perspective of AWNA's clients as well.

"Even with all the work that Bill Draayer did for the AWNA, when I started in '82, it was still a pretty small business that only had a couple of employees, one of whom was part time, and an office in a strip mall in southwest Edmonton," says Merrell. "But by 1987, we built it up, adding a few staff, getting people marketing and selling, conducting market research and readership surveys, building the business end up mostly. And we developed a program called Market Analyzer, which started in

Dennis Merrell, executive director of the Alberta Weekly Newspapers Association (1982 to present)

the early '90s and is the fairly powerful tool that allows anyone who wants to know anything about any of our markets—any demographic information about any community, a complete snapshot of that community. And that helps if you're going to look at buying advertising in newspapers."

More recently, the AWNA has incorporated a digital archive into its operations. "Newspaper editions are searchable back to 2003, giving our clients quicker access to their advertisements. The service also gives readers the ability to subscribe to their favourite community weekly online or to search past archives, for a small fee," Merrell says.

"At the same time, we started expanding into more education, training and seminars for the paper. And for the last 20 years we have had a weekend-long symposium. That's our biggest annual event, with over 150-plus staff showing up. We've really got more involved in helping the newspapers become even better at what they do. That's become more of a focus."

Locally, individual newspapers found themselves in the midst of some major changes, not just in how they produced their newspaper but in the people behind the production.

In the 1980s the personal computer became more prevalent in people's homes and in the work place. "We first started using computers for the business side of things," says Walter Koyanagi, publisher of the *Taber Times* and other newspapers in southern Alberta for more than two decades. "I first set up an accounting system on a computer and then it was a natural that we would use it for our mailing list. And from there, it didn't seem that unusual to use computers for other tasks at the paper."

The task that changed how weeklies and other newspapers operated was something called desktop publishing. Prior to the advent of desktop publishing, all newspapers created their issues in a similar manner. Reporters typed out their story on a typewriter, did a quick edit and handed the hard copy to a typesetter who retyped the article on a Compugraphic, or a similar typesetting machine, that spit out the article on long sheets of photographic paper. The story in this form went through a final edit and proofing with a blue pencil, and the copy was inputted again into the Compugraphic by the typesetter. The final copy was then run through a wax machine and the story cut and pasted into the layout of the paper. These sheets were photographed to create a film image— a thin plate was "burned" and that plate was mounted to the press so the newspaper could be printed.

How long the issue stayed in the office of the newspaper during this process depended on the kind of equipment a newspaper had in its back shop. Some papers completed their work to the layout step and sent the

AWNA Board of Directors 1995. Standing (left to right): Al Blackmere, Frank McTighe, Barry Hibbert, Duff Jamison, Greg Foster, Coleen Campbell, Bob Hillier. Sitting: Richard Holmes, Gordon Scott, Joan Plaxton, Hugh Johnston

actual cut-and-paste pages to a printer who shot the negatives, created the plates and printed the newspaper. Some newspapers had the photographic equipment in the shop, so they could shoot a negative of the newspaper and then send it to an outside printer who would "burn" the plate and print the paper. Some even went as far as the plate stage and shipped those off to be printed. And in the 1980s, a few newspapers kept complete control of the process and printed their newspaper using their own web presses. These newspapers also acted as printer for many of their contemporaries.

But in the mid-1980s, with the development of the Apple Macintosh computer and desktop publishing programs such as Newsroom, Pagemaker, QuarkXPress and others, the world of newspapers changed dramatically. Reporters still typed their articles, but instead of using a typewriter, they used a computer keyboard and a word-processing program. All editing and proofreading could be done on screen, although some newspaper editors prefer to print out a hard copy for editing and proofreading purposes. Furthermore, the reporter or editor could take all the written articles and lay out the entire issue on the same computer. Depending on the type of system a newspaper or printer had, creating film or even plates to get a paper printed was no longer needed. Nowadays, many newspapers do pagination and e-mail the file to their printer.

A process that had taken previously several steps could now be done by one machine and fewer staff. And the speed in which the change occurred was incredible.

"The transition was immediate. We went from one week typing stories on a typewriter and handing it to the typesetter who typed it into the Compugraphic machine so we could slide those sheets into the wax machine and paste them up on the board, to the next week we were inputting our own stories into a Macintosh computer and starting to use that to start laying out the paper," says *Macleod Gazette* publisher Frank McTighe, who was working at the *High River Times* during the switch to computers. "We had Gord Scott, who was George Meyer's son-in-law, and had been the publisher at Taber, training us. He brought in the computers, stayed with us for the week, got us going, taught us a little bit about templates and stuff like that and left us on our own."

Fortunately, typesetters still had jobs because, despite the arrival of computers in newspaper offices, outside contributors still used typewriters, and for several years afterward, many newspapers continued to design the local ads using the cut-and-paste style.

But considering how major this technological shift was, Alberta weeklies adapted rather quickly and easily. "A little known fact is that for one of the very last major revolutions in newspapers, Alberta weeklies were ahead of the curve," says Dennis Merrell. "But adapting to technological change was nothing new to Alberta's weeklies. They had progressed through a number of major technological developments in their history, and another one that would make the job of printing the paper easier and less costly would be as welcomed as the many other ones."

In the early days of Alberta newspapers, from the 1880s to the Great Depression, a large majority of the community weeklies were laid out by hand, each single piece of type in the story—every letter or digit, every head, every space—was placed manually, one by one, to create the finished layout of the page. And many of the machines used to print the newspapers, such as the famous Washington hand press, were hand operated. So just getting the paper laid out and printed involved many hours of backbreaking and tedious work. Publishing a newspaper was literally a labour of love.

"Before the 1960s, the only people who were involved in community papers were printers. It was the only way you could be a newspaper publisher, if you had that printing operation so you could actually print the paper," explains Merrell. "Before web technology and the big printing operations, you just had to crank that sucker out in your back shop, and you didn't want to have to go to someone to get that done, you had to be in control of that. So it was the printer, printing the business cards and the letterheads for the local folks, but by the way, they also put this paper out. The real business was the actual printing operation; it was always that way. But they were newspapermen, they loved to put the newspaper out and write those editorials, but it was more of an avocation than a real job."

Although the Linotype machine was invented in the late 1800s, its use didn't really hit Alberta weeklies until after World War I. It was a hot and time-consuming process in which operators sat in front of a keyboard with the copy set to be typed sitting in front of them. Once the machine was set for the required point size and line length, a pot was heated to 550°F, hot enough to melt the lead, which was forced, through a pumping action, onto the brass to create the "line of type."

"The idea was to get the molten lead poured as quickly as possible, before the metal started to freeze (harden). It was allowed to cool; then the clamps were removed, the lead plate was peeled from the matrices and presto! (assuming all went the way it was supposed to) you had a lead cut of whatever size," wrote George Meyer in his book, *A Prairie Publisher*. "This was then mounted to a block of hardwood or lead, and planed to a thickness known as 'type high,' which was nothing more than the same height, or thickness, as foundry type or a Linotype slug."

All the type in a page form or anything else meant to print using Letterpress had to be type high, with leads and slugs for spacing, and anything else locked into a steel frame called a chase, by quoins on the opposite side of the chase. Each quoin could be tightened against each other so that the entire, heavy lead page could be lifted onto the bed of the press. On the press, anything that was type high was inked and would come in contact with the paper to create the printed pages.

"It was a very complicated and exacting process, as was the very nature of hot metal printing as practiced during the machine age after the industrial revolution," wrote Meyer. "I soon fell in love with the Linotype, even though it was one of the most frustrating machines in the world to operate. That is not surprising considering it needed constant maintenance and adjusting, and especially when one further considers it had something like 2500 moving parts, all of which could wear out or go out of adjustment at any time. In addition to setting type, a Lino operator soon became a fairly competent machinist. The older the machine, the more that could go wrong, and the one in Nanton was quite old. Still, we were able to keep it going for most of the time."

Despite the mechanical issues, a Linotype could set type much faster than a person setting it by hand. Almost all the newspapers in Alberta used a Linotype by the time of the Great Depression. Although the type of

Ken Patrige (1961) was the editor of the *Camrose Canadian* and was prominent in both the Canadian Weekly Newspapers Association as well as the Alberta Weekly Newspapers Association.

machine used to print the newspaper varied from paper to paper (primarily sheet-fed presses because this was the technology at the time), the use of the Linotype was the industry standard for more than three decades.

Then, on January 20, 1955, the *Taber Times* made history by printing two pages using the offset method. Officially, this was the first time that any part of any newspaper in Western Canada was printed using the offset method. Some have noted that using the offset method may have been a Canadian first as well, but the claim has never been confirmed. Since offset was a photographic process and did away with the hot lead to set the type, it was known by the term "cold type." And because it didn't involve a machine with thousands of pieces of type, a mistake could be easily rectified, so offset proved to be faster and less expensive.

"How does offset work in the newspaper field?" wrote Arthur Avery, publisher of the *Taber Times* in a letter to Ken Patrige, co-publisher of the *Camrose Canadian*. "In the case of the *Taber Times*, we have for just over a year and a half been using a Harris 22 × 24 offset press for producing a two-page pictorial section in the '*Times*' and we are now averaging one of these two-page sections every other week and find that sales of papers at the newsstands goes up considerably when a pictorial section is included in the paper. More pictures is what every newspaper has to have these days, and we have chosen to use the offset press to accomplish this and are quite satisfied with the results being attained, when some reasonably priced method is devised to quickly give the publisher justified lines on either film or paper, it will give the offset work a still better boost."

Alberta newspapers such as the *Taber Times* and others, led the way in the use of offset, not just in Alberta but in the rest of the country.

"Our local weekly community papers were adopting cold type in the '50s and the '60s, many years prior to the larger dailies, which didn't really completely go over to cold type until about 1970," said Dennis Merrell. "A lot of people wouldn't think that small papers would be ahead of the curve, but in fact, they were. The smaller organization like a weekly newspaper is better equipped to turn on a dime and change than a larger one like a daily."

The next major technological change in newspapers was in how they were printed. As said earlier, almost all weekly newspapers were printed using sheet-fed, letterpress machines before the 1960s. But web-press technology, in which large rolls of paper are fed through the press and cut to size at the end, changed the way newspapers operated.

Throughout the history of Alberta newspapers, some publishers made deals with others to get their papers printed. These kinds of deals allowed one publisher, who had a better printing operation, to

Ralph Klein giving a speech at the AWNA "Zoofari" Convention, Calgary, 1996

supplement its income, while allowing the other paper to save money by not making a major capital investment. But as mentioned, until web presses became part of the Alberta weekly industry, most newspaper publishers printed their own newspapers; it just made more sense, physically and economically.

"And instead of the core business of a newspaper publisher being the printing side, things changed," said Dennis Merrell. "You now had many publishers saying that their core business was the newspaper. They would still take in the printing jobs, but instead of printing these jobs in the back shop, they farmed them out, so by the mid-'70s they were really just agents for printers, most weren't doing the printing any more. Even so, when I started in the early '80s, there were still a lot of printers among our members, but today there are really only a few, and they are the ones with the big web press operations. And even that is beginning to change again because if you have to be in that game, you have to be big."

So back in the mid-1980s, weekly newspapers adjusted quickly to the new computer technology the same way they adjusted to other technological changes like Linotype, cold type and web press. But there were still concerns.

"When desktop publishing came around in the '80s, everyone had to chuck their old machines out," says Merrell. "And the big fear then was that anyone could start up a newspaper in their home office. You could, theoretically, but you still needed to know what package to put around it to make it sell because it's a business. So desktop publishing didn't put community newspapers out of business like people would think it would."

The process of putting a newspaper together and printing it may have changed—the same way it had changed many times over the history of Alberta—but the actual fundamentals of producing a newspaper and how the people who created that weekly were connected to the community did not.

In the early days of the Alberta newspaper industry, anyone who had the money to buy a press, the patience to set type and the strength and stamina to run a press could found a newspaper. But in the end, a large number of these early newspapers folded or were sold, and their founders faded from memory. Being a newspaper publisher in Alberta involved more than technology; there was, and is, always something else.

"One thing about our newspapers that really sets us apart is the strength of our membership, the involvement of the editor and publishers in their communities and being not just something that covers the community but something and someone that is part of the community. It's also about being involved in the industry, furthering the industry and ensuring we're on the leading edge," says Merrell. "Members in Alberta have always been a bit more proactive in that kind of stuff, more so than their counterparts in other parts of the country, and it's something that our papers pride themselves on. And I think it does get back to the pioneer maverick mentality that's always been there in Alberta. The 'let's get it done' kind of attitude prevails to this day. For example, if you bring up an idea for a program in another jurisdiction, the first step will be to get a government grant, while in Alberta, we'll look to ourselves first. I mean how can we editorialize in our newspapers about government waste or mismanagement if we're part of the problem. So it's always been that sense of 'we do it ourselves, our way.' And that's the characteristic going back to the beginning of the province in the late 1800s when newspapers started. I don't think it's changed that much. It just seems to be one of the things that defines Alberta and that fuses itself into the fabric of community newspapers as well and how they present themselves."

So while the Alberta newspaper industry braved many technological advances that some said would bring about their demise, another change was in the air before the province turned 100 years old in 2005. Alberta newspapers had a reputation since their early days of being do-it-yourself maverick pioneers, but the industry would be transformed because the ownership of newspapers in Alberta, and in all of Canada for that matter, was becoming much more centralized.

~

Monday-night Fights

For a large part of its history, Alberta went to the polls on different days of the week. Local elections to choose the mayor, members of town council and the school board were usually held on Wednesdays. Provincial elections to choose the premier, the governing MLAs and those in the Opposition were usually held on a Thursday.

For Alberta's weekly newspapers, several of which came out on Tuesdays and Wednesdays, these varying election days presented a dilemma. Most of the province's election results were a week old by the time the next issue of the local paper came out. A few newspapers tried to remedy the situation by releasing early editions of the newspapers whenever an election was held. But that tactic was only a temporary solution.

And changing a publication date because of an election had ripple effects in the operation of the newspaper. For example, if a community newspaper had a publication date of Wednesday, that meant the paper was printed the Tuesday night. So the deadline for news items would be noon Tuesday, giving the editorial staff enough time to edit the stories and determine the layout of the newspaper. Advertisers also had a booking deadline so the newspaper's designer had time to design and place the ad according to the advertiser's specifications. So moving the publication date but a single day would require major adjustment to that week's newspaper.

The AWNA appealed to the provincial cabinet on various occasions to change the date of municipal elections to Mondays, but most of their appeals fell on deaf ears. Although several of the rural weekly newspapers were supporters of the Socred government throughout the mid-1900s, the slights against them by the party's founder William Aberhart in the 1930s were not completely forgotten. The province wasn't going to change something as important as an election at the behest of an association of newspapers editors and publishers.

But the AWNA didn't back down from the numerous rejections. In 1980, association member George Meyer was elected mayor of Taber and saw a different approach to the situation. He presented his dilemma to the Taber town council and they drew up a resolution that was presented at the next annual convention of the Alberta Urban Municipalities Association. It seemed that many small-town councillors and mayors were also unhappy with having week-old election results appear in the local paper, so the resolution passed. So instead of having just the AWNA push the idea of Monday elections to the provincial government, pressure was also coming from an association of Alberta mayors and town councillors.

On October 17, 1983, Albertans, for the first time, went to the polls on a Monday to select their local governments. The results of the elections appeared in their local weekly newspapers either the next day, Tuesday, or on Wednesday.

Six years later, on March 20, 1989, Albertans went to the polls to select members of the Legislative Assembly. It was the first provincial election ever held on a Monday, and since then, Monday provincial and municipal elections are standard election policy in Alberta.

CHAPTER NINETEEN

Consolidation of the Newspaper Industry

THROUGHOUT THE HISTORY OF ALBERTA community news, it wasn't entirely unusual for a newspaper publisher to own more than one newspaper.

"Owning more than one paper and expanding out to places like Vauxhall and opening the *Advance* there just made sense," says Walter Koyanagi, former publisher of the *Taber Times, Vauxhall Advance* and the *Coaldale Sunny South News*. "With those papers in line, we had a nice triangle of serving communities around Taber."

However, from the late 1980s through to the early part of the 21st century, the ownership of Alberta newspapers started to change. While independent "family-owned" newspapers were still part of the landscape, their numbers began to decline. Over time, companies like Bowes Publishers, Great West Publishing, the Hollinger Group, Sun Media, Black Press, Alberta Newspaper Group, Westmount Press and others, began to change the make-up of the AWNA.

"My tenure with the AWNA has been 30 years, and when I started in 1982, 75 to 80 percent of the newspapers could be called independents, owned by one person or a group such as a family in the community it

Barry Barnes and Coleen Campbell (*Taber Times*) at the 75th AWNA annual convention in 1995

served," explains Dennis Merrell. "And now in 2012, the number of newspapers owned by independents is just under 50 percent. And I would say we are one of the last bastions of free and independent newspapers in the country because for years, BC, Ontario, Québec and Atlantic Canada have been almost completely controlled by large groups...80 to 90 percent of their papers are owned by a handful of five or six media and newspaper groups. In Alberta and Saskatchewan, about half of the papers are still independent operations, so the Prairies are still a good place to be for an independent publisher."

The prevalence of larger corporate groups owning weekly newspapers in Alberta came about because of two developments. First, many of Canada's dailies were, and still are, owned by corporate interests such as Southam, Thomson, Hollinger, TorStar and, later, Canwest and Sun Media. Several of these companies were looking to expand their media holdings, but since Canada has a limited amount of communities that can support a daily newspaper, the large media chains had to either buy an existing newspaper from a competitor or start their own newspaper, as the Sun Media chain did in the late 1970s and early '80s, and as Conrad Black did with the *National Post*.

Many of these companies then realized that weekly newspapers were solid business performers because of their close community connections and their stable subscription and advertising base. And with national advertisers seeking new markets in which to promote their products, community newspapers were seen as a reliable investment and a means to expand media holdings in previously underserved markets.

The major players in corporate community newspapers came from a variety of sources. Some came from the east, like Hollinger, Post Media and Sun Media. Others came from the west over the Rocky Mountains such as Black Press and Glacier Newspaper Group. And they also came from within Alberta, such as Great West Newspapers of St. Albert.

But the consolidation of weeklies didn't stop with these companies buying up newspapers. Over time, the companies began buying their competitors, and Alberta weeklies consolidated even further. Bowes was sold to Sun Media, which was purchased by Quebecor. As a subsidiary of Sun Media, Bowes bought all the newspapers in the Westmount chain in 1998, making this group the largest owner of Alberta weeklies, with over 30 newspapers.

Glacier developed two partnerships in order to be involved in the ownership of almost 30 Alberta newspapers. The first partnership was a 50/50 share agreement with Great West of St. Albert. Despite the even split of shares, Great West CEO Duff Jamison holds majority vote and manages the operation. Glacier also owns 59 percent of the Alberta Newspaper Group, which owns 19 newspapers in Alberta.

Alberta weeklies were also at a pivotal moment in their history. As had occurred a couple of times in the past 100 years, newspapers in

From left to right: Peter Schierbeck (*Fairview Post*), George Meyer (*High River Times*) and Ossie Sheddy (*Drumheller Mail*) at the AWNA 75th anniversary celebration, 1995

Alberta were hitting a generational transition. Some of the industry's publishers had been overseeing their newspapers since just after World War II and the following 15 years. Many of them were approaching the age of retirement, and though they loved being newspaper publishers, for some, it was time to move on or take life a little easier.

"That's what happens," says Dennis Merrell. "The publishers all start reaching retirement age, and nobody from the next generation was interested in newspapers. There were no children or grandchildren or nieces or nephews interested, so that's it. And the reality is, if that had happened, some of these newspapers still could be independently owned because now, when you look at other newspapers like the *Drumheller Mail*, that newspaper has been in the Sheddy family for three generations, but fortunately, the current editor and future publisher Bob Sheddy is a young guy and if he wants to continue to operate, that [newspaper] may stay as an independent. *Rocky Mountain House Mountaineer* is the same thing. The next generation of the Mazza family has taken it over, and they aren't close to retirement. Brooks is in there too. The same family has been running that paper since Len Nesbitt bought it for $500 in 1911."

For many of the reasons stated by Merrell, when the major media companies came courting, publishers couldn't resist.

Jack Tennant, who bought the *Airdrie and District Echo* in 1980 and at one time owned six weeklies, most of them along the Highway 2 corridor between Red Deer and Calgary, was one of the publishers who sold to a larger chain.

"It was so time consuming, and I basically got tired of it," Tennant said in an interview for this book. "I was also writing a column for the *Calgary Sun* five days a week, so after 14 years, it was getting to be too much. I just kind of unwound a lot of stuff, and I sold most of my papers to Bob Doull of Westmount, although we kept the *Olds Albertan* and *Innisfail Province*. My partner Murray Elliot was running those, so I was just barely part time."

In 1998, the *Echo* was sold to Bowes Publishers (then part of Sun Media) when Doull sold the entire Westmount chain to Bowes, and the paper is still published by Westmount. The *Innisfail Province* and the *Olds Albertan* were sold in 2005 to the Mountain View Publishing group in a deal that included three other papers: the *Didsbury Review*, the *Olds Gazette* and the *Sundre Round-up*. Two years later, another newspaper in the area, the *Carstairs Courier*, was sold to Mountain View, now part of Great West Newspapers.

The consolidation of several Alberta weekly newspapers being sold to larger chains wasn't a quick process. In fact, the amalgamation of Alberta weeklies began in the 1980s and continued into the early 21st century.

the Weekly REVIEW

VIKING ALBERTA CANADA

www.weeklyreview.ca
twitter.com/vikingweekly

Caribou
Publishing

Canada Agreement #40005387

The town of Viking has been served by a newspaper since the spring of 1910 when the *Viking Gazette* came into existence with Fred T. Phillips as editor. The *Gazette*'s printing equipment was lost to fire in January 1912 and in May 1913. The *Viking News* replaced the *Gazette,* with John W. Johnston of Fort Saskatchewan as proprietor.

Originally, the newspaper was printed by hand, but according to "Remember When?" a regular column authored by H.B. Collier, a large gas-operated cylinder press was installed in 1916, and by 1920, the news office had purchased a Linotype machine.

In February 1978, the first edition of the *Viking Weekly Review* arrived in mailboxes and in stores, established through a partnership of Lane Carrington, Dick Morris and Monte Keith. At its inception, the *Weekly Review* was in competition with the *Viking News*, and in just over a year, the publishing rights to the *Viking News* were purchased by the *Weekly Review.*

The final edition of the *Viking News* was delivered in July 1979, ending a 66-year run for the paper. Just before the purchase of the *Viking News*, Carrington and Morris became the sole owners of the *Weekly Review*, a partnership that lasted until the summer of 1982 when Morris became the sole owner.

Morris purchased the Thor Agencies building, which had previously been the home of the town's bakery, and the paper stayed at that main street location until August 2011 when it moved its offices up the street to its present location at 5208–50 Street, a former main street convenience store.

In November 1993, the paper was purchased by Kerry Anderson and Rick Truss, owners of *The Community Press* in Sedgewick. Immediately after buying the *Weekly Review*, Anderson and Truss updated the office with the latest computer equipment and desktop publishing programs.

In 2005, Anderson became sole owner of the publication, as well as the *Tofield Mercury* and *The Community Press*. At the end of that year, Anderson also founded the *Lamont Leader* based in Lamont—a community that was virtually without any local news source.

In March 2006, the group of four newspapers began publishing weekly publications, as well as additional supplements, printed by Star Press Inc. in Wainwright.

The *Weekly Review, Tofield Mercury, Lamont Leader* and *The Community Press* also publish a monthly insert called the *East Central Times*, which on the second Tuesday of each month reaches a much larger demographic of readers (roughly 35,000).

The *Weekly Review* has won numerous awards and is proud of having been the community leader in fundraising efforts for such worthwhile causes as helping Manitoba flood victims, Kosovo refugees, tsunami aid and Hurricane Katrina victims. Locally, the paper has donated thousands of dollars in free advertising and support since a tragic fire in 2005 destroyed the historic Viking Carena where the NHL's famous Sutter family learned to play hockey.

In 2007, stage one of the new complex was opened, and with strong support from the community, it was named the Carena to continue the legacy and history lost in the fire. In late 2008, stage two was completed, which included the library, meeting room, fitness centre, walking track and playschool.

The *Weekly Review* is currently printed by Central Web in Edmonton and continues its proud tradition of covering events in all the surrounding communities, holding true to the original idea that by calling it the *Weekly Review*, no specific community would claim sole ownership of the publication.

Readers of this column in next week's Camrose Canadian *will be treated to the different views of a different editorial staff.*

There will be new people in both the publisher's and editor's chairs, and we feel sure you'll find their views interesting, stimulating and we hope, debatable.

For over twenty-five years this column has been the product of one writer's imagination, one writer's prejudice, interests and expression. We've tried to keep it interesting, we've tried to make it challenging, we've tried to provoke discussion, or at least, as we looked at circumstances around the community, the province, the nation, the world we live in. We've probably been ultra conservative in some areas, while leaning to unacceptably modernistic views at other times. And on many occasions, we've probably been downright boring.

Anyway, after a quarter of a century, it's probably past the time when readers should be treated to other viewpoints, to other concepts. We know the people who'll be bringing this column to you. We know their principles, their values, their yardsticks. And we're glad to see people of this caliber taking the helm.

–Camrose Canadian, April 2, 1985

The Nanton News *begins a new chapter in its 92 year history today.*

Westmount Press Ltd., which publishes newspapers in B.C. and Alberta, has bought The News *from Frank and Emily McTighe.*

The News *is the second acquisition in less than a month for Westmount Press Ltd., and its president Bob Doull. Two weeks ago the company announced it merged with* High River Times.

Other Alberta newspapers owned by Westmount include Banff Crag and Canyon, Canmore Leader, Cochrane This Week, Strathmore Standard, Airdrie Echo, Calgary Rural Times *and* Jasper Booster.

No immediate staffing changes are planned at the Nanton News.

–*Nanton News*, February 21, 1995

No more headlines or deadlines for me! This is my last column, editorial, story or whatever you want to call it.

This is the time to be somewhat emotional and to reminisce, about the good times and some bad times that we have had when some unappreciative individuals have made our lives miserable. But I don't want to dwell on it and wash that dirty linen in public on this particular occasion.

As one of the few independent weekly newspaper publishers in Alberta, we did our best to produce one of the finest award-winning quality newspapers with the few resources at our disposal. Many of my fellow publishers have wondered how we have survived all these years in one of the hotly contested markets in the area.

Those reporters who have had the privilege of going through the tough Ladha School of Journalism will testify today that they had excellent training. They obviously cursed me when they worked here and they didn't like what they were told to do; some of them today are working in daily newspapers or television stations across Canada and I am proud to say that their initial training was in small town Morinville under yours truly, originally from primitive Africa!

But the time has now come for us to say goodbye, get realistic and make way for chains like Bowes Publishers Ltd., one of the most progressive weekly publishing groups.

The future of these papers looks bright as I settle in my favorite chair and think about that book I was going to write one day.

It seems that day has arrived. It was nice knowing all of you.

–Mansoor Ladha, *Morinville Mirror,* June 1, 2005

For many in the media industry, the sale of weekly newspapers to corporate interests was of major concern. Some companies had also purchased dailies, and media critics had commented on how corporate interests had changed the editorial direction of the newspapers. In 1996, the *Calgary Herald* suffered through a debilitating strike, one of the reasons being the ideological differences between the editorial staff and the paper's owner, Conrad Black of Hollinger.

So when large corporations such as Hollinger and others purchased weeklies, there was apprehension. Who would control the editorial content and direction of the newspaper? Would having a large corporation owning the local paper sever the connection between the paper and the community it served?

In the end, business stayed pretty much the same. Some advertising increased, and some editors and publishers retired and moved on. A couple of long-time newspapers folded, but that was mostly because they had a competing newspaper in town. And most of the companies' owners, such as Duff Jamison of Great West and the two Bowes brothers of Bowes Publishers, all had their roots in Alberta community weekly newspapers. Even the first newspaper Conrad Black bought, the *Eastern Townships Advertiser*, was a community weekly newspaper.

So whatever the new owners' ideological viewpoints, most of them understood that the connection to the community was one of the key reasons behind the success of a community newspaper. When a larger corporation purchased a weekly in Alberta, one of two things usually occurred. First, if the former publisher/editor retired, a new one was hired and that person moved into the town to become part of the community. Or, if the former publisher/editor was not of retirement age and was still interested in being involved in the newspaper, that person stayed on as an employee.

"It was almost like I was at my own paper anyway, we just had to file some financials once a month. For the most part, they gave us free rein," says Frank McTighe, who sold his *Nanton News* to Westmount in 1995. "I never minded working for the larger corporations. They always treated me fairly. The philosophy was that if you did your job and you did it well enough, they left you alone. It was almost like when I was in Nanton or Macleod, Vulcan or whatever. That said, there's a psychological difference in working for yourself, the hours you put in and the work that you do, it's sort of for you. And I guess that's one of the reasons why I went back to owning my own paper."

"There's not always the same point of view coming from a corporate owner than an independent newspaper, there is no way getting around that. I just follow a pretty simple rule of thumb. Whenever faced with a given situation, I look at what's in the best interests of the many as opposed to the few. And that does sometimes mean that we make decisions on things that are going to benefit the independents because we have 40 to 50 out there, and that's an important constituency to us," says Dennis Merrell. "We have never been an association of 'this is what the large group wants, and we follow along.' We frequently have said this won't work for us and here's why. But we negotiate, and we usually get the larger companies to see our way. Some day we might become only relevant to the independent operator and not to that large corporate guy. It could get to there. But there will always be some services that will be appealing to that large operator; they always like to gather with their peers and to be a part of these newspaper awards to get recognized."

But no matter who owns a newspaper, one thing is for sure.

"The quality of papers has never been dictated by the type of ownership," wrote David Cadogan in the July 2003 issue of *The Publisher*. "Some lone papers have had excellent owners and publishers and editors, advertising sales and creative people. Some have been pathetic. Some groups haven't paid much attention to editorial quality. Others strive for excellence in every aspect of the endeavor. Some papers have achieved excellence in spite of management."

～

CHAPTER TWENTY

The Bowes Brothers

IN THE SUMMER OF 1950, JIM AND BILL Bowes were owners of the *Dresden Times*, a weekly newspaper in southwestern Ontario. Both were veterans of World War II, Jim as a correspondent for the *Maple Leaf*—the Canadian Army daily newspaper that covered battles in Italy, Belgium, Holland and Germany. The younger Bill was a RCAF navigator, flying missions from an airbase in England until he was discharged in 1946. After the war, each Canadian veteran received $7.50 per month of military service plus another $7.50 per month if they had served overseas during the war.

Jim and Bill pooled their war service gratuities to buy the *Dresden Times*. Since Jim was the one with editorial experience—prior to the war and his service with the *Maple Leaf*, he had worked for dailies in London and Woodstock, Ontario—he dealt with that aspect of the paper. Bill's focus was on the business and production side. Both men were considered salt-of-the-earth, hardworking, community-minded individuals who were driven to succeed but without big egos or the desire for recognition. Even as their publishing empire grew, the two brothers retained their reputation as decentralized, family-atmosphere managers without major public profiles. Of course, people knew who they were, but only

From left to right: Lawrence Mazza (*Rocky Mountain House Mountaineer*), with his wife Mildred, and Marilyn and Howard Bowes, 1995

for their paper and their community work; they didn't seek out public attention.

During that summer of 1950 in Dresden, Jim and Bill were talking to a couple of travelling salesmen about the boom times in Alberta. One salesman commented that if he had the money and was much younger, he would buy a newspaper in Grande Prairie. At the time, Jim Bowes was 29 and Bill was 25.

Even though Bill and Jim knew nothing about the area, they decided to make the move west. They sold their Dresden newspaper, and with those monies, decided to look for a newspaper in Alberta. The *Grande Prairie Herald-Tribune* was on the market, so on September 30, 1950, they made the deal to buy it. The brothers named their company Bowes Publishers.

1977 AWNA Executive. Top row (from left to right): George Meyer (*Taber Times*), Peter Pickersgill (*Vulcan Advocate*), Bill Holmes (*High River Times*), Jack Gieg (*Leduc Representative*). Bottow row: Ossie Sheddy (*Drumheller Mail*), Jack Parry (*Rimbey Record*)

Over the next decade, the Bowes ran the paper the same way they ran the one in Dresden: Jim in charge of editorial, Bill in charge of production and the business. During that time, they began the expansion of their company. Their first acquisition was the *Peace River Record-Gazette* in 1953.

Although Bowes Publishers has become one of the largest newspaper publishing companies in Canada, it made its mark in the industry in 1963, when the *Grande Prairie Herald-Tribune* became one of the first newspapers in the country to be printed by the rotary offset method. And when the paper became a daily in 1964, it was the first daily newspaper in Canada to be published using that technology.

By this time, the younger brothers in the Bowes family joined the business both as employees and investors. Howard Bowes of Leduc started his own company, Lynard Publishers, which eventually owned seven AWNA weeklies before being purchased by Bowes Publishers in the late 1980s. As the brothers raised families of their own, their grown-up sons became part of the business. And as the family grew, so did Bowes Publishers. It slowly bought publications in Alberta and outside the province. By 1987, Bowes had 14 weeklies, three dailies and six magazines publishing under its banner. And even though it was the largest privately owned community newspaper chain in the country, the company still retained its family-style operation and preserved the idea of a newspaper being part of the community.

But larger corporations were becoming interested in weekly newspapers, and just before Christmas in 1987, Sun Media approached Jim Bowes, the majority shareholder of the company. By the time spring rolled around in 1988, a $28.8-million deal was struck, with Sun Media acquiring 60 percent of the company. In 1990, Sun Media bought the remaining 40 percent.

In 1999, Bowes Publishers became a subsidiary of Quebecor, the largest media and printing chain in Canada, when Quebecor purchased Sun Media.

Jim Bowes passed away in 1996; Bill died in October 2011. Howard Bowes, a former AWNA president and first recipient of the prestigious Bill Draayer Award in 1983, still lives in Leduc with his wife Marilyn.

~

The first buildings that were eventually to develop into the town of Vulcan formed just a tiny settlement in 1910, but with the coming of the railroad in 1911, growth was rapid, and in 1912, Charles Clark, then owner of the *High River Times*, became convinced that the little centre some 40 miles southeast of High River would soon be large enough to support a weekly newspaper and job printing plant.

Preparations began early in 1913 when a small-frame building on Main Street was acquired. By the late summer, a job press, some type and other equipment were moved in. A newspaper press had not yet been acquired, but on August 6, 1913, the first issue of the *Vulcan Advocate* was published, the type being set by hand and the paper printed at the *Times* office in High River and then sent to Vulcan for distribution. This was the method of publication for a few months until a two-page newspaper press was installed at Vulcan.

The first managing editor of the paper was R.W. Glover, who continued in that capacity until he moved to Calgary in 1919. In 1917 a brick and tile building was constructed on Main Street to house the *Advocate* offices and printing plant. Bert Klebe was the first printer at the *Advocate*, and when a Linotype was installed to set the type for both the *Advocate* and the *High River Times*, Tommy Logan was the first operator and remained here until 1922, when he moved to High River as Linotype operator, continuing in that position until his retirement.

Between 1919 and 1921 there were three editors: F.D. McDannel, A.R. Ganoe and J.J. Duffield. In July 1921, Harry Nelson was appointed as editor, and during his eight years in that position was a great booster for the annual school fair and for all sports. Upon his retirement in 1929, he was succeeded by Tom Whittingham, who was editor until 1932 when he left to become editor of the Cranbrook paper.

In 1932 Charles A. Clark, the founder's son, became editor, assisted by R.D. McElroy, a former resident of Blackie, as printer. In 1932, Mr. McElroy was made editor, and his new assistant was Robert Munro, fresh out of high school. In 1936 Mr. McElroy moved to Vancouver, and Bob Munro was appointed editor, assisted on press day by Jack Anderson who for the rest of the week worked at his father's store, F.M. Anderson & Co. Ltd. Mr. Munro and Mr. Anderson both enlisted for active service in 1941 and, by a quirk of fate, were together in Holland as officers in The Calgary Highlanders when Mr. Anderson was killed and Mr. Munro wounded in the same action.

In 1941 J.L. Findlay came from Trochu to take over as editor when Mr. Munro left, and the same year Miss Lola Bateman (later to become Mrs. Findlay) started as his assistant. From October 1943 to April 1945, Mr. Findlay served in the Air Force, and during this time Miss Bateman acted as editor and got out the *Advocate* each week with the assistance of high school students and other part-time help.

Mr. Findlay again became editor in 1945, with Miss Bateman as his assistant. In February 1946, Mr. Munro returned from overseas, and in June 1946, returned to Vulcan as managing editor of the *Advocate*, with Keith Perry from Manitoba as back-shop assistant.

In 1947 Mr. Munro purchased a half-interest in the *Advocate* from Mr. Clark Sr. of High River. After Mr. Clark's death in 1949, Munro purchased the other half-interest, making it a wholly owned Vulcan business for the first time since its establishment in 1913.

Since 1946, many changes have taken place at the *Advocate*. None of the equipment used in the first post-war years remains. The original two-page newspaper press, augmented in 1959 by a faster, four-page press and only used about two hours a week in its later years, was broken up for scrap in 1968. In the same year, a major development was made in the production of the newspaper by the changeover to the offset method of reproduction. The original SO-It building had been enlarged in 1959 by the addition of a 40-foot concrete block extension, and in 1968 extensive interior alterations, including the building of a darkroom and an office for the assistant editor, were made. Computers now set the type rather than using Linotype, and all production work on the *Advocate* was done in Vulcan. The actual presswork was done in Cochrane.

In 1946, circulation of the *Advocate* was about 600 copies per week; by 1949 this more than doubled to a circulation of over 1300. By 1965, circulation had reached its present 2600 copies per week.

In 1995, the *Advocate*, now owned by Peter Pickersgill, was sold to Westmount Press, a company headquartered in Cochrane. It became part of a 21-paper group serving southern Alberta and parts of British Columbia.

With the change of ownership came new management. Dave Wilson arrived in Vulcan to head the editorial, production, sales and customer service team.

In the late spring of 1998, the *Advocate* again changed hands, being purchased by Bowes Publishers, the largest community newspaper chain in Canada, headquartered in London, Ontario. Bowes is in turn owned by Sun Media, publishers of daily newspapers in several locations, including Calgary and Edmonton.

Technology has made great changes in the publishing business. Full colour reproduction, which first appeared in the *Advocate* in 1996, is one of the improvements that can be most easily seen by readers. Behind the scenes, material is constantly being moved throughout the office and around the country by electronic means. Over the years the staff and management have remained committed to bringing our readers and customers the best possible service.

The *Advocate* is now printed on the presses in Leduc, and in 2001 Wanda Domolewski became publisher until 2006 when current publisher Nancy Middleton stepped into the role.

CHAPTER TWENTY-ONE

Provost and the Ku Klux Klan

DURING THE FIRST WEEK OF SEPTEMBER 1990, a group of individuals held what they called a private event six kilometres west of the town of Provost. Normally, a publication like the *Provost News* wouldn't provide coverage for such an event. But this meeting was different. It was billed as the first Alberta Aryan fest and was hosted by the Church of Jesus Christ Christian Aryan Nations, a white supremacist group led by Terry Long, a farmer from Caroline, Alberta.

During the weekend gathering, the group chanted white power slogans, shot guns into the air and argued with people who were protesting the event. Attendees also burned a 10-metre-high cross, saluting and circling it while wearing white Ku Klux Klan–style robes and head gear.

For the town of Provost, the news was disheartening. "The thing is, we're trying to attract doctors here," said Richard Holmes, editor of the weekly *Provost News*. "This is a heck of a time for this to happen."

Some argued that the white supremacist event should be ignored and that the Aryan Nations was only a small fringe element of the total population. It was also said that reacting to the gathering, either through protest or media coverage, would only give the KKK free publicity and bring legitimacy and new members to their organization.

Ed Holmes (*Wainwright Star*; *Provost News*), date unknown

George Holmes of *Provost News*, date unknown

But instead of ignoring the event, the *Provost News* put it on the front page under the banner headline: "Community Members Protest Aryan Gathering." The paper even published a few photos, including one that showed three white supremacists standing underneath a Nazi flag. The editorial of that week's paper explained the reasons for the coverage.

The weekend just ended will go down in local history as one that many will want to forget, but in fact it's one that should always be remembered.

The reason why such an incident should be remembered is that the atrocities of Hitler's war on humanity, specifically against Jews, Gypsies, Masons and others who were the "wrong" colour and religious belief—must never be repeated.

The people who congregated west of here from points mainly unknown in Alberta and Saskatchewan, although holding shotguns were not fearful. It was the ideas being promoted that are fearsome. They do, of course get to hold on to their views, however distasteful, but the rest of the general public get to display their views as well. And we're proud to say that many of them did—from school students to other members of the community at large, to a death camp survivor and a veteran from Calgary who drove here by himself.

In this community, there are no grandchildren of those who went to fight Hitler. Personal memories of the war of 50 years ago are beginning to grow dim and radicals again question if a Holocaust was even held. This is exactly why incidents held over the weekend should be talked about, discussed and dissected, so that the new generation can see the truth instead of hearing tiresome slogans.

No one knows exactly how many people died in the terrible Holocaust in WWII. Numbers are not the issue in this editorial. Even if only one man, woman, or child is gassed or

News Office
Burns, 1940s

The Provost News editor fought in World War II and then came home to experience this shortly after the war. A fire destroyed The News office and two other businesses on Main Street, Provost. Fire broke out a couple of doors down the street following a late night card game, the story goes. All records from *The News* were saved as were these type cases piled out on Main Street. The Linotype was pulled out of the shop with the help of mules but unfortunately the entire machine tipped over on its side. Time was spent rebuilding the machine and with the help of an *Edmonton Journal* employee, the paper was late coming out by only a few days that week.

The office of the *Provost News* was destroyed by a fire in the 1940s

persecuted simply because he or she is not affiliated with the people professing "white power," another crime is recorded.

See you on November 11.

—*Provost News*, September 4, 1990

For the next couple of weeks, the paper received countless letters to the editor from around the country and continent, condemning the white supremacists and praising the community for protesting the cross burning and other actions. "We showed through pictures, news stories, letters to the editor and an editorial that the community was not in favour of this type of event taking place near our town," says Richard Holmes, editor of the *Provost News*. "Ignoring such people and their dubious activities might have been seen by some as perhaps allowing or sanctioning such an event. Some people tried or maybe hoped to ignore a certain dictator with appeasement in the late 1930s in Europe but of course history shows that usually does not work. The issue was best to be met head on and have the light shone [on] it so that it could be dissected and dealt with, not left covered up."

As a result of the media coverage from the *Provost News* and other media outlets, the Alberta Human Rights Commission implemented an inquiry into the events of September 1990. Richard Holmes was asked to testify, to give his view and recollection of what occurred that weekend.

The head of the Aryan Nations group, Terry Long, also testified at the inquiry. But halfway through his testimony and cross-examination, the inquiry broke for the day. Long refused to return to the inquiry. When an order for his arrest was issued, he fled to the United States. The inquiry continued on without Long, and in its final decision, ruled that signs and symbols meant to discriminate against classes of people based on their race, religious beliefs, colour, ancestry or place of origin were illegal in Alberta.

"The Aryan Fest was a shocking event in the history of Alberta," declared board chairman Timothy Christian. "The blatant display of signs and symbols redolent of racial and religious hatred, bigotry and discrimination challenge the very foundations of our society. You can't walk around with a Ku Klux Klan outfit on and you can't burn crosses and you can't fly Nazi flags and you can't go around shouting 'Seig heil' or 'Death to the Jew.'"

So because the Aryan gathering wasn't ignored, because media outlets like the *Provost News* covered the story, Alberta took a major step in reducing the promotion of hatred in the province—laws that still stand today.

On September 12, 1991, one year after the event, *Provost News* was awarded the AWNA Award for Best Local News Story in Alberta.

CHAPTER TWENTY-TWO

One Hundred Years and Beyond

THE PROVINCE OF ALBERTA turned 100 years old in September 2005. Considering the significance of that milestone, editorial comment in Alberta community newspapers was relatively muted. Most newspapers relied on photos or recaps of centennial celebrations in their communities to honour the occasion rather than making some type of comment on the editorial page. Alberta's centennial was a significant celebration and was covered as such, but in the end, it didn't really affect or change the day-to-day lives of Albertans.

> Pincher Creek's centennial weekend got underway on Alberta's birthday, Sept. 1, as the Kootenai Brown Pioneer Village was packed for the opening reception of the Pincher Creek Centennial Exhibits and Centennial Social.

> "I had no idea we had so many pioneers in Pincher Creek, this is overwhelming and I'm so delighted to see this many people out," Historical Society president Colleen Casey-Cyr said to open the evening's festivities.

> Casey-Cyr estimated that there were nearly 300 people in attendance to honour those families who first put down roots in Pincher Creek over a century ago and to explore

the new exhibits, which included such artifacts as pictures,
swimsuits, books, quilts phonographs and much more.

"This evening has just been wonderful," she said.

–Pincher Creek Echo, September 6, 2005

The lack of opinions about Alberta's centennial on the pages of week-lies did not mean that the papers had lost their fervour for editorial comment. In the tradition of their forefathers, they didn't hold back their opinions in response to events occurring throughout the nation and the world.

It was with great sadness that we at the Local Press listened
to the news of the terrorist activities in the United States on
September 11. What lies ahead is anyone's guess.

Our hope is that the lives which were lost in the attack will
be revenged, but not by killing other innocent people. It is the
very masterminds behind the terrorist activities who should
pay—not the civilians in those countries who don't support
those individuals.

President Bush declared a war on terrorism, saying the
United States will attempt to put an end to terrorism. That is
a very large goal. Terrorism will exist for as long as there are
people with different religions, beliefs, values and ideals. To
put an end to terrorism could almost mean putting an end
to humanity.

–Claresholm Local Press, September 19, 2001

The experience can only be described as humbling, standing in
the Edmonton Garrison Lecture Training Facility surrounded
by soldiers saying their final goodbyes to their families before
being shipped out to Afghanistan for six months.

The LTF is not the sort of place people would choose as a place
to say goodbye if they had their choice. At once you are struck

by the starkness of the building. It's essentially a large barn-like structure with bare cement floors with only provincial flags draped on the walls for adornment.

But it's a stark place, too, where they're going, largely treeless and full of rocky mountains.

The faces of the soldiers leaving were a mixed bag of emotions. Some looking genuinely excited to be going as if this would be the adventure of a lifetime. Others, usually the more experienced soldiers looked more resigned to the fact that they'd be gone for six months to one of the most dangerous places in the world.

The striking fact was that they were going.

How many of us have ever truly risked our lives for the good of others? Canada seems to have a split personality when it comes to our military. We lavish praise upon them for acting as peacekeepers and we tell them how well they represent our country and Canadian values abroad and yet no politician in recent memory has lost an election vowing to cut military spending.

In some ways we treat our military like an aged grandparent we visit only when we need money. We feel there are more important things in our busy lives than to make the effort to think of them daily. We know when we need them they will always be there.

Perhaps what is most amazing is that many, if not most, of the soldiers heading off to Afghanistan joined the Canadian Forces during an era of cutbacks and base closures. They joined knowing that the military was underfunded and neglected by the federal government. They joined anyway.

And now, knowing all the potential dangers they will be facing, they are going anyway.

Good luck. God bless. Come home safe.

–Morinville Mirror, August 4, 2004

There is a reason newspapers have comment pages. The editorial page and the letters to the editor page offer staff and readers (alike) the opportunity to engage in conversation.

Unlike the other pages of the paper, the comment pages offer opinions, not facts. By reading other people's opinions and offering your own by submitting letters to the editor, you can be part of the debate that shapes our community.

There is often reaction to opinion pieces printed on these pages heard around town, but rarely do those comments find their way to the paper where they can become part of the debate. Open and direct communication is a fundamental component of our democratic system and the cornerstone of the free press. By presenting alternative viewpoints, you broaden the debate and engage more people in the issue at hand.

Right now we're drawing closer to a federal election that could have a dramatic impact on our province and community. In the Macleod riding, voters have a full ballot to choose with each of the major parties represented. Yet most of the talk so far has been coming from the candidates.

For many years now, Alberta has remained a Tory bastion regardless of the way the rest of the country had voted. Perhaps that explains the apparent apathy surrounding the election. Perhaps everyone is content to reinstate the status quo for another round. Yet we at the Nanton News can't help but wonder why—if everyone is apparently so happy with the status quo—many of the stories we print each year deal with people who are in one way or another upset with the government. People who don't like the Conservative stance on big oil in our province, people who are angry with continual social program cuts in the face of a growing surplus, people who disagree with the current government's approach to the environment.

Like the editorials and columns in the newspaper, the current political scene appears mired in the same apathetic swamp that hampers action in favour of coffee table bickering.

This is your platform. Join the debate and help shape our community. As the renowned American author Kurt Vonnegut Jr. one said, "What's worse: being persecuted for speaking your mind, or having all the freedom in the world with nothing to say?"

—*Nanton News*, September 25, 2008

The world was going through major cultural and technological changes, and these changes affected Alberta's weeklies. The Internet and e-mail allowed instantaneous communication around the world, creating an information explosion in which websites offered comment and coverage of news literally seconds after the events had occurred.

The first edition of the *Vermilion Standard*, dated May 19, 1909, marked the beginning of a newspaper that has been recording the news of the town and quoting the views of its prominent citizens for over 100 years. The stories that unfold on each page both reveal and conceal the history of the *Vermilion Standard* itself—the paper has published hundreds of thousands of stories but rarely gets a chance to tell its own story. The history of the *Vermilion Standard* is inextricably connected to the history of Vermilion, of Alberta and of Canada.

When Sextus Ruthven Pringle Cooper, founder of the *Standard*, arrived by rail in 1906, Vermilion was little more than a dusty section of prairie littered with tents and haphazard log buildings. His prior newspaper experience in Manitoba compelled him to invest in a partnership in the town's existing newspaper, *The Signal*, owned by William Bleasdell Cameron.

Before arriving in Vermilion, Cameron had survived the Frog Lake Massacre, a pivotal moment in early Canadian history.

By 1908, the town was growing up around the fledging newspaper. Cameron and Cooper worked side by side while schools, churches and electrical plants popped up around Vermilion. Roads were laid, and professionals, such as teachers, doctors and engineers, began to flock to the small settlement east of Edmonton.

Cooper was prompted to start up his own paper, the *Vermilion Standard,* when he bought a failed printing plant a few miles away in Mannville. Cooper and Cameron continued to assist in each other in emergencies until Cameron retired from the newspaper business to write an acclaimed account of the Frog Lake Massacre titled *The War Trail of Big Bear.*

In 1910, Cameron moved to Bassano, Alberta, and Cooper's *Vermilion Standard* became the only newspaper in town. For 44 years, Cooper served as owner, publisher and editor of the small paper. His presses printed the story of the 1918 Vermilion fire in the department store, bank and hardware store that burned to the ground, and the paper also covered the reconstruction of main street. The fire added to the sadness of a town already mourning the deaths of several young men who never returned home from the war in Europe.

The paper's offices were one of the few downtown businesses that did not burn. As such, it is still part of the expanded building the *Vermilion Standard* uses today and is one of the oldest buildings in the town.

Up until 1937, the staple of Vermilion's economy was agriculture. Stories about farm practices and crop advice abound in the early pages of the *Standard*. In August 1937, the paper broke the story of the new oil field discovered in the Vermilion area. A few weeks later, the *Globe and Mail* picked up the story. A vital part of the economy of Vermilion, and of Alberta, had begun.

During the hailstorm of World War II, Vermilion's airstrip was classified as an emergency landing field and was charted on Allied air maps. The decision to build the airstrip was made in December 1941, shortly after the Japanese attack on Pearl Harbor. A salvage depot opened a few weeks later as part of the town's war effort. The oil fields around Vermilion also made a significant contribution to oil supplies sent off to the front. A year later, oil workers were disappointed when the oil conditioning plant in the area was closed. Crude oil had to be sent west to be treated after the plant's closure.

Over the next 10 years, the *Standard* reported the arrival of a RCMP detachment, the sale of the Vermilion creamery and the appearance of a large pothole on the town's main street. Radio arrived, and peace was negotiated with the Axis forces. A Vermilion woman, who refused to let her name be published in the paper, spotted a flying saucer. An enormous water tower was erected, and a salt plant was constructed 50 miles (80 kilometres) away.

Cooper celebrated his golden wedding anniversary with his wife, Myrtle Louise, and left the running of the *Standard* to his four sons shortly thereafter.

Polio reared its ugly head in Vermilion in 1952. Seventeen cases were reported, and five of Vermilion's children succumbed to the illness. The Vermilion hospital purchased one of the first centrifuges in Alberta to help combat the unnecessary spread of germs in its wards.

In 1963, dial phones arrived in the homes of Vermilion's citizens, and the town was granted the telephone number prefix of 853, still in use today. Four years later, Vermilion acquired what would become a proud part of the community—the fire school opened its doors to its first students.

S.R.P. Cooper passed away in 1964. His sons sold the paper to the Stubbs family in 1973.

In 1976, the *Standard* converted to a "fully modernized" system with a combination computer and printing implement. The office was renovated to accommodate the new system. The town continued to gain modern features when Lakeland Mall opened in 1981. The *Standard* changed hands once again in 1990 when Meridian Printing took ownership.

Meridian ran the *Standard* for five years. In 1995, Bowes Publishers Limited took ownership of the paper. Since the purchase, the *Vermilion Standard* has continued to play a vital role for the 4500 citizens of the northeastern Albertan town. The paper has garnered awards from the local RCMP, town council and school board for its equitable reporting and extensive community coverage.

The *Vermilion Standard* has been the keystone in the arching triumphs of its community for more than 100 years. Every word printed on every page of the newspaper is a piece of Vermilion's history and a foundation for the future. The *Standard* will continue to preserve Vermilion's history, one week at a time.

Readership throughout the weekly and daily newspaper industry dropped to its lowest level since before World War II. Soon, it was predicted, most people would get their news from the Internet, either through their computers or Smartphones. And with the perceived environmental concerns of cutting down trees to make newsprint, newspapers were predicted to go the way of the telegraph or the semaphore as means of obtaining information.

"If you're a weekly editor or publisher of a small community newspaper, those bigger issues are important, but you're also focused on getting that paper out every week and that's the reality, your biggest fear, you need to keep relevant and keep publishing week in and week out and keep in business for the next five to 10 years," said Dennis Merrell in 2009. "If you look at the media family, dailies are finding it harder and harder to stay relevant with what's happening with the Internet and everything else that crowds in. Having said that, community newspapers are still very relevant."

"It's the coming thing, the Internet, there's no doubt about that," says Jack Tennant, owner and publisher of the *Cochrane Eagle,* founded in 2001. "I can go into the newsroom and have a reporter sitting there on the Internet, and he can tell me what's going on in China. That's great. But then I say 'Get off your ass, I wanna know what's going on across the street.' Because what's going on down the street is that little Jimmy Smith has just scored his first goal in Cochrane. And no website is going to tell you that. The local paper can, and that's our strength and that's what we should be doing. But the other side of the coin is photography. We now have access to every reader who has a digital camera, and we get hundreds of photos submitted every week."

The AWNA took the lead with the Internet by establishing AWSOM (Archival Web Search for Online Media), the first online searchable archive of community newspapers in the country. Developed in the early part of the 21st century, AWSOM allows readers, for a subscription fee, to

Left to right: Ben Huckell (Innisfail), E.L. Horton (Vegreville) and Charles Clark Sr. (High River), in the late 1930s or early 1940s

download digital editions of their local paper and others in the archive in order to keep up to date on events in their district and around the province. Advertisers can also access the archive to keep track of campaigns and placements, and to see what their competitors are doing and respond accordingly. And because the AWNA coordinates national advertising placement, AWSOM can also deliver digital tear sheets (copies of the ads as they were printed in the paper) to these advertisers. The archive has been so successful that it has been expanded nationally to include over 200 newspapers from every province and territory in the country.

AWNA Executive at 1981 convention. Top row (left to right): Trev Harris (Beaverlodge), Oliver Hodge (Bow Island), Al Willis (Stettler), Peter Schierbeck (Fairview). Front row: Paul Rockley (Claresholm), Byron Keebaugh (Lloydminster), Barb Wright (Stony Plain) and Gary MacDonald (Sylvan Lake)

~

Community newspapers are also changing the way they present information to their communities. "In the small community, there is always going to be a need and a role for someone to disseminate that information about what's going on in that community, whether it's a combination of printing the paper and more use of websites with streaming audio and video of local events," says Merrell. "And most of our members have video cameras, and they are not just covering the event, they are videotaping the event so it can be put up on a website. There are adjustments that have to be made, and the ones that are successful in doing that will still be around 10 to 20 years from now."

In the over 120 years since Frank Oliver began the first weekly newspaper in Alberta with the *Edmonton Bulletin*, Alberta weeklies have had to contend with a lot of major issues, not just events of world history but also those that shaped the history of the province. And in our time of instant information from every corner of the world, news from local sources was seen as more important.

"For the news of the day-to-day living in a small Alberta community, you're going to find that on the pages of the community newspaper," said Frank McTighe, publisher of *Macleod Gazette*, in an interview for this book in 2009. "Many readers still like getting a newspaper, but our method of delivery will evolve a little bit. We will still have a newspaper for a long time, but the expectation is that we will do more online as time goes on. The local newspapers will find their place and that place will be as the local information provider, and however we do it, through our website, sending it to your cell phone, whatever, we will do that as time goes on and as demand grows. And as a bit of an old dog, being out here in the weekly newspaper industry for over 28 years, I'm excited that there is something new coming along. But the fundamentals are important; you need to be able to write a good news story, you need to be able to shoot a photograph, you need to be able to edit. Those fundamentals are so important no matter how you provide that information; you need to have the skills to be a good journalist in order to do a good job whether you do it online or in print. And that's going to hold up."

But the story of Alberta's weekly newspapers doesn't end there. Not by a long shot.

~

CHAPTER TWENTY-THREE

Bust and Boom

IN THE FEW YEARS AFTER ALBERTA'S centennial celebration, the province was in the midst of an economic boom. Housing prices were skyrocketing and high oil prices were sparking exploration and expansion of established reserves. In the United States, Alberta's oilsands were seen as a safe and friendly alternative to the oil supplies they got from such sensitive areas as the Middle East, Venezuela and Africa. The province's population grew at unprecedented rates, giving Alberta the highest net interprovincial migration rate in Canada. In 2007 alone, Alberta's population increased by over 100,000 people. The government surplus was estimated at $8.5 billion in the spring budget of 2008. Times were good.

However, in the summer of 2008, Highwood Communications, the former exclusive ad-purchasing agency for the government of Alberta, went bankrupt. For over 10 years the company had the contract to buy advertising for all of the Alberta government's departments and agencies. The company not only placed the ads, but it was also given government money to pay for the ads. Highwood Communications lost the contract following the election of Ed Stelmach as the new premier. And when the company declared bankruptcy in 2008, it still owed money to Alberta's media outlets, including almost $800,000 to members of the AWNA.

AWNA past presidents at the AWNA 75th anniversary in 1995 (left to right): Jack Gorman, Lawrence Mazza, Oliver Hodge, Jack Parry, Peter Pickersgill, Howard Bowes and Trevor Harris

The loss hit the AWNA hard because almost every newspaper in the membership ran government ads placed by Highwood. The AWNA either did not get paid for those ads or it had to accept a lower payment, more than 60 percent less than the rate it was supposed to be paid.

The AWNA weathered the storm, but more trouble was on the horizon.

From 2001 to 2007, North America experienced a major housing bubble. Prices rose to almost unimaginable heights, and banks (especially those in the U.S.) were keen to ensure that almost everyone who wanted a mortgage could get one. But by 2007, the housing bubble in the United States burst, putting that country's financial system into a fragile state. The result was that much of the world suffered an economic meltdown, the largest and most damaging financial crisis since the Great

Depression. In Alberta, oil prices dropped from $147 a barrel in July 2008 to $55 a barrel in November. Alberta's expected $8-billion surplus turned into a $1-billion deficit. And for 2009, the government's budget predicted a $4-billion deficit.

The downturn in the economy struck many hard, including the media. Sun Media, owned by Quebecor, cut 600 jobs across Canada in 2009, which included journalists in Alberta.

"It all happened pretty quick," says Tyler Waugh, former publisher of the *Hinton Parklander*, a weekly that was founded in 1955 by Kenneth McCrimmon. "Everything was going along great at the end of 2008. It was a great time. We were doing well on the books, pretty well with readership, we just had our Christmas party and we were on a dizzying high. But early the next week, I was informed to start letting people go. I got an e-mail one morning, out of the blue, that I pretty much had to let someone go, at that moment. And that same day found out that composing was going to be centralized. I was also running the *Edson Leader* at the time, and between the two of them, I had let go half the staff in the space of four months.

"As a publisher I understood the business side of things, I get why it had to be done," adds Waugh. "But the way it was done was deplorable."

George Brown, the president of the AWNA at the time, returned from his holiday to find out he was out of a job as publisher of the *Beaumont News* and *Devon Dispatch*. Layoffs also occurred at the *Grove Examiner/ Stony Plain Reporter, Camrose Canadian, Lacombe Globe, Sherwood Park News, Strathmore Standard* among other papers. Composing for most of the Sun Media newspapers was centralized at a plant in Drayton Valley.

The *Nanton News* remained, but its office in town was closed and operations were centralized out of the office at *High River Times*, 27 kilometres away. The worst news was that two long-standing and award-winning community newspapers, the *Jasper Booster* and the *Morinville/ Redwater Town and Country Examiner*, were closed.

It saddens me to write this, as I'm [sure] it saddens our readers to know that we will no longer be bringing the news to their doorsteps.

While none of us here were expecting the closure, perhaps we should have taken a bigger hint from the economy surrounding us.

My biggest regret is the unfinished business, knowing that we will no longer be able to tell the many stories of our community. I know for a fact that countless stories exist out there. Hockey playoffs continue, graduations inch ever closer and yes, crimes continue to be committed. It's all the way the world works. News will happen regardless of anything else, and we will no longer be able to bring it to our valued readers.

We took pride in being your newspaper. We told your stories, while at the same time keeping you abreast of the latest happenings in and around your community.

I can say with all honesty that we would not have done a thing differently, sometimes circumstances dictate that certain decisions are out of our hands and unfortunately, this is one of them.
—Morinville/Redwater Town and Country Examiner,
March 11, 2009

I never thought that I would be writing in the last edition of the Jasper Booster *with tears in my eyes and a feeling that something great, something so many different people cared about over the last 46 years just died.*
—Jasper Booster, March 11, 2009

The *Jasper Booster* was founded by Fred Donovan in 1963. It changed ownership over the years and became a part of the Sun Media Group in 1999.

The *Morinville/Redwater Town and Country Examiner* was created in November 2008 through the merger of two long-serving community newspapers, the *Morinville Mirror* and the *Redwater News*. Both had been owned for more than 25 years by Mansoor Ladha, who had bought the papers in 1979 after moving to Canada from Tanzania.

Whatever people may say about the death of newspapers in our society, the discussion often obscures the fact that as a popular commodity, newspapers hold a special place in peoples' hearts and play a vital role in society, especially in a small communities like Morinville and Redwater. In a city, one has alternative media such as television to cover the news, but in smaller towns, it is the community newspaper only which is there to cover the local happenings.

The weekly newspaper reporter, usually fresh from university doing his first job, is hard at work covering town councils, school boards, chamber of commerce and municipal district meetings, most of which are ignored by our friends in the dailies unless there is something controversial happening. The sports reporter covers hockey and other sporting events so that local teams can get coverage in the papers and our up-and-coming sporting heroes can get a boost in their careers so they can go to the next level.

Even as a publisher, I was summoned at home, many times on weekends or in the evenings, to come and take a picture of the president of the local Lions Club, for example, since he forgot to inform us about the plaque that was to be presented by the district governor to one of his members. You just can't say no as one could in a city. That's what community journalism is all about, the publisher of a weekly is on duty 24 hours a day, seven days week. The contribution of a local newspaper to the community is enormous.

After running the two weeklies for 25 years, my wife and I had run out of steam, but we had left the papers in excellent economic shape. As one of the few independent weekly newspaper

Left to right: Marion and Byron Keebaugh (*Lloydminster Booster*) and Mildred Mazza, at the AWNA's 75th anniversary, 1995

~

publishers left in Alberta, we did our best to produce an award-winning, quality product with few resources at our disposal in one of the most competitive markets. We realize times have changed now and even corporate ownership and paternalism couldn't save the papers.

I lament the demise of these community newspapers, which have fallen victim to the tough economic environment, whether it's because of dwindling ad dollars or poor readership. The community has lost its best friend, one who always stood by its side, and shared their happiness and sadness.

–Mansoor Ladha, *Calgary Herald*, March 2009

Ladha wasn't the only person to mourn the closure of some weeklies and the layoffs.

It's a sad day for weekly newspapers in Alberta. The Jasper Booster *and the* Morinville-Redwater Town & Country

Examiner *were closed after many years of publication. Sun Media that owns 200 weeklies across Canada are busily closing weeklies and downsizing dailies. They have eliminated more than 600 positions, including a multi-awarding winning editor/publisher, George Brown of the* Devon Dispatch *and* Beaumont News *and current president of Alberta Weekly Newspapers Association.*

I've never been a big fan of big corporations. I'm a believer that small and medium size businesses are the true engine of economic growth and are absolutely integral to small towns and sparsely populated rural areas.

Big corporations, such as Sun Media buy up small weekly newspapers. They then shave costs by cutting staff and using canned copy for news. They pack up the profits and move them into their city operations or into their own jeans. When the small town paper has been bled dry, they close it.

Newspapers serve to educate, to inform, to entertain and to inspire debate. Local papers can report on issues that affect the area they cover. They announce and report on local events. They are an effective way to buy and sell, or find work.

There are few independent papers left. Most newspapers in Canada are owned by three big corporations. The East Central Alberta Regional Review *published by Coronation Review Limited is one of those privately owned papers. Publisher Joyce Webster has been running the business for 24 years.*

It can be argued that newspapers are passe and that everyone will get their news online. The Review *believes that there is room for both, hence our initiative this past year to put our paper and advertisements on-line at www.ecareview.com. We regret that we are unable to provide local reporters on the ground in every community, but always appreciate and encourage freelance writers and communities themselves to submit stories. We try to focus on provincial issues more than federal as we believe the provincial government has a much greater impact on our individual welfare and wellbeing.*

We are committed to the region we serve, and its because of our dedicated staff, our advertisers, our freelance writers, a host of volunteers and most important, you the reader, that we are able to continue to grow the content of our paper. We believe that being informed takes more than a 30-second spot on TV news or Dave Rutherford's daily rants, and so we will continue to provide in-depth news content both on-line and in print.

Democracy only exists when an electorate is informed and there is a forum available to enable a free exchange of varied ideas. We believe this forum is best served when there are viable and independent on-line and print newspapers.

–Coronation Review, March 26, 2009

The closures of several major U.S. newspapers and layoffs throughout the industry again brought forth the argument about the death of newspapers.

Instead, something else happened. Sure, times were tough for newspapers, including Alberta weeklies. But then again, when has publishing a weekly newspaper ever been easy? As Mansoor Ladha wrote, "Even in good times, advertising is hard to come by in smaller communities as residents in those towns somehow have to be educated about the benefits of advertising. Many of them believe that because they are located on Main Street, Alberta, they do not have to advertise. The argument being that everyone passes by the Main Street and sees the store, so there is no need to advertise, yet the hockey teams and the Scouts would expect the newspaper not only to give free coverage, but also donate towards cups and trophies for their tournaments."

Selected best community newspaper in Alberta — AWNA

St. Albert
Gazette

www.stalbertgazette.com   Serving St. Albert and Sturgeon since 1961

Newspapers are the mirror of a community, linking neighbours and friends and reflecting the happenings that define it. St. Albert, founded as a humble settlement by a priest on a holy mission nearly 140 years ago in 1861, was no exception.

Over the years, the community hosted a handful of newspapers that quickly came and went, until the 1960s, when one would become the mainstay for St. Albert readers.

Details of St. Albert's early journalistic enterprises are sketchy, and not without some ink-soaked irony.

The *St. Albert Gazette,* for example, was launched on June 17, 1961, and has kept humming on the presses ever since. What most readers may not know is the *Gazette* had actually made its début in St. Albert many years before, albeit for a very short run.

The first issue hit the streets in 1908 but also became the last, according to historical references, because of a lack of printing equipment. A second paper, the *St. Albert News,* was up and running by the spring of 1912 and was publishing as late as 1916, but how regularly is unclear. But it did outlive a more flamboyant competitor, the *St. Albert Star/L'Etoile*, which published in English and French, reflecting a desire to serve both cultural facets of a growing community.

The *Star* was put out by Joseph Lafranchise, who also printed a paper in Morinville and, in 1914, moved to St. Albert with his wife Rosanna. The *Star* was printed each week, and although most of the articles were similar in content, the French version also contained news that tended to sympathize with that culture, running articles dealing with the protection of French language rights in Western Canada and other related issues.

The paper, which occasionally ran articles promoting St. Albert as a good place to live and shop, primarily filled its pages with events from across Canada and even the world, with stories filed from as far away as Paris, France.

One article dealt with the exciting saga of a threshing machine crashing into a bridge over the Sturgeon River, while another celebrated the first run of streetcars across the High Level Bridge in Edmonton.

Advertising, always the lifeblood of a newspaper, helped the *St. Albert Star/L'Etoile* survive, through vital clients such as St. Albert pioneer and businessman Fleuri Perron, who owned the community's general store and splashed bargains (eight pounds of onions for 25 cents, men's suits from $4 to $20) across a full page each week.

But after the *Star* folded sometime later that decade, there would be no local paper for a generation. Instead, St. Albert readers read the *Edmonton Bulletin* and the *Edmonton Journal* until 1961, when Wim and Evelyn Netelenbos began producing the resurrected *St. Albert Gazette*

from their home on Sunset Boulevard.

The Dutch-born couple toiled alongside their children to produce the weekly paper. It was printed on 11 × 17-inch sheets and folded to 8½ × 11 inches and filled with bits of local news. On June 17 of that year, the first issue rolled off the presses, featuring a sketch of Father Albert Lacombe on its front page.

In 1966, ownership of the *Gazette* changed hands and became the venture of another family, the Jamisons.

Originally Ponoka-based, publisher Ernie Jamison bought the *Gazette* as a vehicle to distribute another publication, the *Western Weekly*, a magazine supplement running with weekly newspapers throughout Western Canada. "I needed to increase the circulation to support the publication," Jamison recalled. "I could see I had to be some place where I could get the *Western Weekly* going."

Growing up in Edmonton, Jamison had worked at the *Edmonton Bulletin* selling ads during the early part of his career. As a child, he had become familiar with St. Albert because it was a stopping point when his family visited relatives in Athabasca each summer.

He saw potential in the *Gazette* and approached Ronald Harvey, a well-known St. Albert resident who owned the paper, asking if he would sell. "I talked to him and he said if I wanted to buy it, he'd be interested." The men struck a deal over a cup of joe at a downtown Edmonton coffee shop and, in 1966, Ernie and his wife Shirley, who took on editing duties, put out their first issue with a circulation of 1200 papers and six staff.

St. Albert, a town of about 7000 people, had few businesses at that time, so the Jamisons relied heavily on advertising from the city next door. "All my advertising came out of Edmonton. I could see the businesses there would like to have St. Albert's business."

At the same time, Jamison looked to the north to bring in trade for St. Albert businesses. He clinched a contract with the Municipal District of Sturgeon to put out a paper containing the minutes of council meetings.

District correspondents were hired to collect bits of news in their regions, and the *Sturgeon Gazette* was born in the late 1960s. The local correspondents became a vital part of the paper, Jamison said. "They might even take pictures with their own cameras."

Quarters were cramped upstairs in the Perron Street building, which housed *Gazette* operations. Piles of paper tape from the Frieden typewriters, used to set copy, littered the floor. Jamison recalled one day when Dr. William D. Cuts stopped in to drop off a news tidbit. He left with one of his own—a long snake of tape caught on his shoe. "He was walking through it and he walked down the street with this stuff dangling."

By the time St. Albert Centre was built in 1979, the city's population had mushroomed to 29,512 people and the *Gazette* had moved to bigger digs, first across from the Bruin Inn and eventually to its current home on Chisholm Avenue in the Campbell Business Park.

Printing the paper had always been problematic because it had no press of its own and was at the mercy of other area presses to do the job. That meant it often printed late. Early on, Jamison took it to presses at Wetaskiwin, Edmonton, Edson and even North Vancouver to print. "It was a real challenge," he recalled. "It had me on the run."

In 1980, the *Gazette* reached a milestone by installing its own press, which has been added to many times since. "I thought, we've finally got it made, everything under one roof," said Jamison.

The *Gazette*'s editorial flavour rested largely with Shirley Jamison, a strong believer in doing a job up right, said her husband. "That's the only way she would do it. She was up on all the major things."

When she arrived to help her husband with the newspaper, Shirley began penning editorials each week, an unusual luxury for readers. "Very few weekly newspapers had editorials. She was so far ahead. We tried to put out the best paper editorially and in make-up, which we succeeded in doing," said Ernie. Over the years, the *Gazette* has won numerous awards for its quality and unflinching scrutiny of community issues.

Ernie Jamison passed away in 2003. The next generation of Jamisons—Sarah, Mary, Sandy and Duff—now publish the paper. They took on Southam and its successor Hollinger as a partner in Great West Newspapers and began to expand the business.

At the end of 2005, the Jamisons bought out Hollinger and took on Glacier Media Group as a partner in Great West Newspapers.

The Jamisons have acquired land in St. Albert's Campbell Business Park and are in the process of moving to a new office and production facility in May 2012. They now own 21 papers, mainly in Alberta, and the printing plant is a 24/7 hub of activity.

While the *Booster* and *Examiner* were closing down, other weeklies were starting up. When the *Jasper Booster* shut its doors in 2009, it didn't leave the town without local newspaper coverage. The *Jasper Fitzhugh*, which was founded in 2005, still offered local news on a weekly basis. The difference between the *Booster* and the *Fitzhugh* was that local residents independently owned the *Fitzhugh*.

Similar events were occurring in towns like Hinton, Strathmore, Cochrane and others, where local residents or former employees of the corporate-owned weekly began acting like the pioneering publishers of the early years of Alberta weeklies by starting and running their own newspapers.

> *There are a few things that should be made clear right from the beginning about the* Voice, *why it was started and what to expect from our humble staff. This was started with the belief that there was a call for a quality, locally-owned weekly newspaper here in Hinton. After researching the independent newspaper community and what may be required for a new business, a decision was made to take the plunge and put chips on the table.*
>
> *With that said, there are still incredibly talented and passionate people working at the* Hinton Parklander, *a long-standing publication that we are sure will remain for many years to come. Our start up should not be perceived as disrespect to their continued professional efforts and appreciated personal contributions to our community.*
>
> *Our new beginning is not about what we left behind, and more about what we want to create—both for ourselves and for the community we have called home for so many years.*
>
> *Our pillars are quality, service and community, with a focus on accountability and active citizenship.*

Former AWNA presidents: Back row (left to right): Paul Rockley, Peter Schierbeck, Gordon Scott, Howard Bowes, Peter Pickersgill, Al Blackmere, Richard Holmes, Lawrence Mazza. Middle row: Bryon Keebaugh, Coleen Campbell, Al Treleaven, Joyce Webster, Hugh Johnston. Front row: George Meyer, John MacDonald, Jack Parry, Oliver Hodge

Our editorial product will support those who advocate for progressive change, highlight local triumphs large and small and draw as much thoughtful attention to those things we must improve as a community.

This first issue has been thrilling, and exhausting, and we're excited to see our labour of love out and about in the hands of the public. We are a small, but dedicated crew at the Voice, *with the hopes of growing as your familiarity and faith in us grows. Yes, we are few. But as Margaret Mead once wrote, "Never doubt that a small group of thoughtful, committed citizens can change the world. Indeed, it is the only thing that ever has."*

Welcome to your Voice.

–Hinton Voice, June 25, 2009

Opening new, independently owned newspapers seemed the logical response to what had been occurring in the weekly newspaper industry during the first decade of the 21st century, when the major corporations closed a large number of weekly newspapers across Canada. Don Sinclair worked for Bowes Publishers and after watching old newspapers close and new ones open, he posted this on his website in 2009:

My congratulations to the latest venture in Strathmore. Long may it prosper. As publisher after publisher bites the dust and more and more publications are being managed by a single publisher living in another community, the window of opportunity for former employees to compete with Quebecor opens wider.

Having been in the weekly and small daily game from 1962 until my retirement in 2001, I have an intimate understanding of how a paper in a small community works. And as former Executive VP and COO of Bowes Publishers for a dozen years, I was instrumental in acquiring many of the papers Quebecor is set on destroying. A weekly is only as good as the people who work there and the publisher, editor and ad manager are key members who liaise with the community every single day. Unlike a major city daily, these people know everyone in the community due to their positions. Relationships are formed at the council meeting, the county meeting, the chamber of commerce meeting, the hockey rink, the curling club, the minor hockey league, the local school, the local pub and dozens of other places too numerous to mention.

The staff in total become part of that community, led by the publisher. When you tear the heart of that relationship out of a community by removing key staff members and managing from afar, you leave a void in that community.

And when a new publication comes along, with a few familiar faces from the days they felt the paper represented them, the loyalty is instantly transferred to the new publication. And so are the advertising dollars.

Even former newspaper folks who pretty much left the industry in the '90s returned to the business of owning and running an Alberta weekly. "My son and I kicked around the idea of a weekly newspaper for a couple of years and then in 2001 we decided to start the *Eagle* in Cochrane," explains Jack Tennant. "It's still fun, that's the main thing. I'm just having fun, and when you love and enjoy what you do, you never have to go to work. It's a challenge, of course, but I do like working with young journalists. I tell these kids you can't make a mistake I haven't made. So let's just get on with it, do your best and we'll talk about it some time."

So even though times were tough before 2010, Alberta weeklies still continued to publish, week after week, the stories and lives of the community they served, be they a newspaper owned by a major corporation or by a local publisher.

"Newspapers will do well if they do what they are supposed to do: reflect the community. And I think that if nothing else, if you are a good community newspaper, you will be successful," says Tennant. "The worst thing we did in the newspaper business is let the bean counters in the newsroom. That's not the driving force that keeps us going. If you're wondering why readership is down—if you don't give people something to read, then the readership is down. If the readership is down, then the revenue goes down. Journalism hasn't changed, the mechanics of it has, with computers and everything else, but it still reflects the community that you serve. You can be a community leader in some ways, but you also have to be a community reflector."

"I love newspapers, I love community newspapers," says Tyler Waugh, editor/co-owner of the *Hinton Voice*. "We just brought in a new journalist and I tell them this is the greatest job in the world. Everything you've done that week is there in print. You get a lot of kudos for it but everything you do is in the public eye, even the mistakes you make. Even if you get a name wrong, it's usually the things like that that will kick you in the butt when you least expect it. But my favourite part of the week is picking up the paper every Thursday morning after it's been printed. The first thing I do every Thursday morning is read through that paper."

"The interesting thing though, the needs of the community hasn't changed that much," says Frank McTighe, publisher of the *Macleod Gazette*. "If you read the weekly paper of 1908 and then you read the weekly paper of 2008, you can see the similarities in what they did, which was to report on what was going on in the district. And that's what made the community paper successful for all those years. And even though we do it now on fancy computers, and we e-mail our pages to press and all that, the fundamentals of what makes a good community newspaper hasn't changed. I think they're the same as they were when C.E.D. Wood and Si Sanders were putting out the paper in a canvass tent in Fort Macleod. I like to think that we write a little bit better and some of our opinions have evolved a little bit, but really at the heart of it, we're trying to cover and reflect the community as best we can."

The newspaper industry and the province has gone through major changes and upheavals since Frank Oliver printed his few sheets in 1880, but some things haven't changed. Albertans are still considered independent, self-made types who are open to new ideas, people and concepts, even if they are a bit resistant to political change. Most of the economy is still based on the province's natural resources, be it agriculture, oil and gas, timber or mining. And the role of Alberta weeklies is still to reflect the communities in which they are situated.

-30-

About the Author

Photo by Maki Blasevski

❀

Wayne Arthurson is an Aboriginal freelance writer in Edmonton, Alberta. He has written professionally for over 20 years, and has worked fulltime as a journalist, editor, communications officer and an advertising copywriter. He has written 100 articles, four history books and three novels during his career.